To Aann'e Carl,

Enjoy!

Michele

MY HUSBAND'S KEEPER

A MEMOIR

MICHELE ARTIZ SMITH, J.D.

Print ISBN: 978-1-09830-220-7

eBook ISBN: 978-1-09830-221-4

Knowledge brings power.
Power brings hope.
Hope brings smiles.
Laughter is the best medicine.

DEDICATION

This book is dedicated to the departed mind, body, and spirit of all those suffering with dementia—and to all those amazing people who care for them and go on loving them. This book is especially dedicated to my husband, Dr. Coral Smith, who must suffer this relentless illness.

Life is a circle of happiness, sadness, hard times, and good times. If you are going through hard times, have faith that good times are on the way.

—Buddha

FORWARD

This is a remarkable, superbly crafted memoir.

It is the journey of a strong-minded, warmhearted woman as she travels through the tragedy of her husband's diagnosis of dementia using faith, courage, clarity, understanding, and inspiration. She shows examples of early, middle, and late stage symptoms and how she developed an action plan for both her husband's future and her own. This revealing story shows that, when her world was divided by an ocean of illness, she made plans for the future: miracles do not come about by hoping, but by action. Often, we think we are not up for the task at hand. But life's challenges will prove you to be the super person you may never have thought you were.

I am inspired by her attitude and her tenacious determination to move forward in the midst of making life-changing decisions that were some of the most difficult in her life. This book inspires and motivates, but, above all, it will hopefully help others facing their own journey in dealing with a partner after a diagnosis of dementia.

Robin Lerner, licensed clinical social worker

CONTENTS

CHAPTER ONE

Getting To Know Us

WOW! WHAT A handsome man standing with America's finest in full-dress military uniform. I think I am falling in love all over again.

My husband Coral and I had been married for several years, and that day was a special day: he had been promoted to Commander in the United States Navy. He was standing erect with his peers vertical and motionless with the others, all regimented and in full military dress.

My admiration for him was limitless. He looked as though he could play the lead in any James Bond film. He was my knight in shining armor and had more charisma in his little finger than most men have in their entire body. He stood there straight as a stick, like a fuse waiting to light yet, there was a calmness about him that seemed to reflect calmness in the world.

My strapping six-foot-two-inch-tall guy had always been athletic and a dedicated jogger way before the popularity of gyms. True, I have always found him irresistibly striking. Some of my gal friends have said he is an Adonis. No, not really girls! Well, maybe. I don't know—perhaps they're right.

Happier times at Hearst Castle gala with special friends.

Coral and I had recently returned to the United States after living in Spain where he graduated from the University of Granada School of Medicine. We were living in the San Diego area. He was looking forward to his Ophthalmology internship at Balboa Naval Hospital and was exuberant about being a part of this branch of the military. (He had served in the Air Force and was also in Vietnam prior to this Navy duty, but that was some years before we knew each other.)

Everything was new to us after being out of the country for the previous five years. We were excited about being back home and looked forward to starting our lives and setting up housekeeping. We had the whole world in front of us in those early years, and there was not much that could interfere with our future plans that we could not handle. We had the recipe for happiness forever after. Without a crystal ball, we could not look into the future of our lives and see the devastation that would enter. That was our beginning together which led to a stable, loving relationship for many years to come, until that changed years later.

The biggest challenge of our lives would surface when my husband, then in his seventies, was diagnosed with memory impairment in 2012.

After visiting the neurologist in 2015 we received the official diagnosis of Vascular Dementia. It is considered the second most common cause of dementia after Alzheimer's disease. There had been clues before that diagnosis that something was not right. Why a neurologist? Because he specializes in diseases of the brain and nervous system?

If you, at random, speak with almost any stranger on the street, you will discover only six degrees of separation between a healthy brain and one that is not. We all know someone in the family battling a lengthy and difficult struggle with dementia or Alzheimer's disease. Worldwide, at this time 50 million people are living with Alzheimer's and other dementias. Every 65 seconds in the United States, someone develops the disease. One in three seniors dies from this disease and dementia kills more people than cancer.

Dementia is the loss of mental function in two or more areas—such as language, memory, visual and spatial abilities, or judgement—severe enough to interfere with daily life. Dementia itself is not a disease but a broader set of symptoms that accompanies certain diseases or physical conditions. Before dementia became a common part of our vocabulary, the term senility was commonly used. The two most common forms of dementia in older people are Alzheimer's disease and multi-infarct dementia (sometimes called vascular dementia). These types of dementia are irreversible, which means they cannot be cured.

My husband experienced memory loss, confusion, personality and behavioral changes, impaired judgement, difficulty communicating as he struggled to find words, and the inability to care for himself as the disease progressed.

This book is not about dementia, but about how dementia impacted our lives. It is about life: our life, my story, my journey sharing what it was like for us in those final years. How I, with my lack of knowledge and my inexperience, navigated from first receiving this diagnosis to those final years leading up to his going into memory care. I share my frustrations and inabilities, my uncertainties of what to do next, and how I moved forward with what had to be accomplished to meet both our needs. I will let the medical experts write about dementia. Most of those books go into the details of the disease itself.

Nothing prepared me for the challenges of having a spouse with dementia. I was catapulted into the complexities of his illness and the negative effects this would have on both our lives. Sometimes life becomes an impossible situation and gives a tremendous blow. At other times, the miraculous will happen. We must learn to let go of the life we have planned to allow for an unknown plan that is waiting. Who would have ever thought this would be our new beginning after almost 50 years together as husband and wife?

Coral and I met in the enchanting city of San Francisco, California, back in 1965. We were married two years later, on a Saturday, in the Swedenborgian Church. The following Monday, we were on a plane flying to Europe where Coral would be continuing his medical studies.

When we met, he was attending the California Podiatry School and had completed two of his four-year medical requirements to become a Podiatrist. He was also working a couple of part- time jobs in order to pay the rent in his shared apartment with two other Podiatry students and pay for his education.

American medical schools were competitive and expensive. It was necessary for him to work while going to school, making it challenging to maintain the 4.0 GPA required by most American medical schools. That meant he would have to look at foreign medical schools if being a medical doctor was that important to him, which it was.

He had friends who were doing very well after graduating from the Podiatry School, but he wanted more than restricted duties in a hospital just dealing with the feet. He wanted to be able to heal the body as a whole. After investigating Mexico's medical schools, he turned to Europe as a resource to accomplish his dream of becoming a medical doctor.

I shall never forget our first trip to Europe and my impressions of the adorable storybook city of Luxembourg. I had never seen anything as charming as this city. It was green and magical, and it seemed as though at any moment Hans Christian Anderson or one of his storybook characters would pop up. We traveled on to Belgium, where Coral interviewed with a medical school. However, the language spoken in the schools was French, requiring him to take a year's classes in French so he could follow instructions in the classes. Coral, at age twenty five, felt losing a year learning a language would take him too long overall. This did not fit into his time table, so we forged on and traveled to Spain, applying to other medical schools. Southern Spain is where we spent the next five years of our newly married life together.

Naïve girl that I was, I did not understand the concept of traveling as a nomad. I brought all my personal possessions in ten suitcases, along with a large steamer trunk that had already been shipped ahead of time.

We made a stop in Barcelona and Madrid; but, we found the medical schools there to be overcrowded and the political climate one of unrest. In general, we thought a smaller city would be better (if you could call Granada a city in the 1960s), as one could remain more focused on one's studies. The University of Granada School of Medicine also had an excellent reputation.

When we left the train station in Barcelona, we shared a train car accommodating six people, sort of like what you might see in the movie *Murder on the Orient Express.* The seats were cushioned and comfortable.

Once we boarded our train, I glanced out the window at the train on the tracks next to us sitting in the station. To my amazement, the passengers were sitting on hard wooden seats with hard wooden seat backs, without any cushions to add comfort for a long journey. I suppose the train dated back many years, perhaps to around the 1930s, as the hard seats should have been a thing of the past. I had only seen such train seats in old movies dating back many years.

Our belongings were packed in suitcases; but many locals had their possessions and other personal effects wrapped in a blanket.

Another surprise that caught us off guard was there were no services on our overnight train and it never occurred to us that we might die of thirst while on this overnight trip or that we needed to bring a lunch along. This was before the popularity of water bottles. September is still very warm in Spain. Although the windows in our compartment could be opened, one of the ladies in our car said she could not take that much air coming in. This made the rest of us suffer, since it was uncomfortably warm in the enclosed compartment.

We also shared our compartment with a man who had a wine *bota* bag and kept offering us a drink each time he took one. A bota bag is a traditional Spanish liquid receptacle made of leather or goatskin. Well, we were not going to drink from the container of a stranger anyway. During the night, every time he took a drink, he would tap us on the leg when we were sleeping and, once again, he would offer us a drink, and we would politely say, "No, gracias." This went on all night long.

Eventually, the following day, the train made a stop somewhere in the middle of nowhere, and someone from one of the villages was selling soft drinks in a barrel. Coral very respectfully went to buy some of these desperately needed beverages only to be too late: he found the fellow had sold the very last bottle. So much for being the courteous gentleman that he was, thinking *ladies first*. No, not next time, ladies—Beware!

So, without relief, we were really on the verge of desperately needing hydration. As it turned out, Coral looked out the window and noticed off in the distance a small structure with a rather large Coca Cola sign. We were once again hopeful, as it appeared all he had to do was run over there and, if we were lucky, purchase something to drink. He took off running while the train was at this stop; but, when he got closer to the shack, he realized it had long ago been abandoned and really the only thing left intact was the Coca Cola sign itself. As he was returning to the train, as fate would have it, the train started up and was moving forward on the journey to Granada. He started running towards the train and people in our compartment, as well as those in other train cars, were yelling out the open windows, "Vamos, hombre! Vamos!" which means "hurry up" or "come on" in Spanish.

The train was picking up speed, and Coral was running as fast as he could. I was thinking, *what the heck. Oh, boy: we are in trouble now. What will happen if he does not make it back to the train?* We were just married, and it was too soon to be separated. He was running faster, and the train was continuing to pick up speed on our journey south. Oh, my: sheer panic was setting in. Well, thankfully, he made it back to the train. But he did not have anything to drink, and he had just been running in the heat of the day to catch the train. We were desperately in need of water. Being so thirsty, we were tempted to drink from the old guy's wine container. No, not really!

Keep in mind, these stops were not routine station stops: they were just stops out in the middle of farm country. If there was a village nearby, we never saw one. A person with a barrel could sell some drinks to the train passengers; it must have been some prearrangement between the train conductor and someone from a nearby village—at least this was my guess.

Coral, my very polite husband, burst through the door, knocking little old ladies and anybody else out of the way. It was a good thing he used to play tackle football! He finally bought several drinks, and we found some hydrating relief that saved the day and our wellbeing. It took some effort and some rudeness, but at least we were not going to die of thirst.

Upon our arriving in Granada, I looked out the window at nothing but agricultural land and open space and said, "Are you sure this is our stop? Perhaps it's the next stop?" After all, I was a big city girl and thought there must be several stops, surely not just one, not realizing then that this was the one and only stop. It was a city, but it was rural to me, especially after coming from San Francisco. It was nothing like Belgium or the cities of Madrid or Barcelona.

We eventually settled in Granada, on the Iberian Peninsula. We were lucky enough to find a newly constructed apartment for around $40.00 per month—no, that is not a typo—and room for all my San Francisco attire in the 10 suitcases that we had lugged all over Europe. Over the next five years, we enjoyed the view of the Alhambra with the famous Sierra Nevada Mountains in the background, which were internationally known for the wonderful skiing.

Then, the population in Granada was about 155,000 people living in and around the city. By 2015, there were more than 240,000 people. Like most other cities, Granada had changed dramatically and had become much more of a city than the large backward pueblo town it was when we lived there in 1960s.

The architecture of the city was a mixture of grand classical buildings and tumbledown old houses. We soon became accustomed to the old relics that looked like they had either fallen apart with time or had been bombed out during World War II. Spain was not then a part of the European Union like many other European Countries, so their economy was not strong at all. That's why the nice new apartment was only $40.00 per month.

We saw locals riding their donkeys, donkey-drawn carts hauling produce, and sheep being herded down the main streets. Another captivating sight were the gypsies traveling in caravans, as well as camping on the ground around their fires for cooking along the unpaved roads.

The country was still under the rule of Generalissimo Francisco Franco, who was viewed by the world as a dictator. Franco was the Spanish general who ruled over Spain as a military dictator from 1939, after the nationalist victory in the Spanish Civil War, until his death in 1975. This dark period in Spanish history is commonly known as *Francoist Spain*, and it was brutal. Before his death in 1975 at the age of eighty two, he restored the monarchy in King Juan Carlos Bourbon I (the grandson of Alfonso XIII, the last king of Spain before the abolition of the monarchy in 1931). He led the Spanish transition to democracy we know in Spain today. Juan Carlos was born in Rome, Italy, during his family's exile. The Bourbons are in power today, and their rule dates back to the Fifteenth Century.

There was a great deal of poverty, a multifaceted concept which included social, economic, and political elements. There were people begging in the streets—mainly gypsies, but Spaniards, as well. Spain had a very low opinion of gypsies. Spaniards would say they are not prejudiced at all, that if you are born in the country of Spain, then you are as Spanish as they are. But they disliked the gypsies immensely and had no reservations voicing their dislike.

In the 1960s, both Madrid and Barcelona were modern cities with lots to do and plenty of culture. Granada was country and backward without paved roads or paved sidewalks, but drowning in historic sites and history.

It rained for nine out of twelve months our first year in Granada. This required walking along the shoulder of the streets in mud and mud puddles, with cars splashing you as they drove past on the cobblestone streets. I was glad I had my knee boots from my go-go days to keep my feet dry.

It was easy to spot a widow, as many women wore black from head to toe: black shoes, black stockings, black dress, and often a black scarf. Spanish women were always dressed and ready for the next funeral. Yes, you spoiled American ladies, once a widow in this part of the world, your wardrobe color is black for the rest of your life.

Most people bathed only once a week. Riding the public city bus for transportation was nearly impossible in the summertime. The smell of garlic-ridden body odor took our breath away. We found ourselves giving up and getting off the crowded bus to walk the rest of the way home.

When we first arrived, we found that the tradition was that a young woman would go out with a friend or chaperone rather than alone. Perhaps that was because of the annoying cat calls. When I was out shopping alone, the wolf calls were awful. The men would say *guapa*, which means "pretty" or *que quiero*, meaning "I love you." It was extremely annoying. But I guess it was better than being in Italy, where the men would circle women on the street and pinch their bottom.

The majority of the male population was short. I towered over almost everyone, as I am five feet, ten inches tall. We noticed something else, which was rather sweet: even men in military uniform would walk down the street holding hands. This was not a gay thing; it just meant "this is my best friend," like what we gals used to do. Being such a dog lover, I saw the animals were not well treated, and many roamed independently along the busy avenues. I wanted to bring them all home with me. Recently, however, when we returned to Granada, it appeared that nearly everyone had a dog as a pet, like the rest of the world. In the summer, I wore dresses, but, in the winter, I often wore slacks. When I went shopping, the women would point and laugh at the strange foreign lady wearing slacks, as that was almost unheard of: the majority of women wore dresses, not pants.

The irony was that, within the five years we resided in Spain, we saw a dramatic change in clothing, and by the time we left in 1972, believe it or not, the younger women were not only wearing slacks but hot pants. Yes, that's right: shorts. Who would have thought it? I suppose that was fashion's Cultural Revolution movement. By then, Franco had left power; when the churches locked their doors, except on Sunday at mass time; the crosses came down off the walls in homes; and the hot pants were out and popular among the young girls.

We felt very safe in Granada. Spain was a police state, and the police knew just about everything going on in and around Granada. Spain had a government that exercised power arbitrarily with an overbearing presence of civil authorities (La Guardia de Civil). If someone had a gathering of several people in their home or piso (the Spanish word for floor or apartment), the police might show up at their door, thinking they were plotting to overthrow the government or cause trouble.

Coral made a friend with one of the traffic officers. Every time we crossed the street when we were in the busy downtown area, he would stop traffic on a dime. He would greet both of us, shake Coral's hand like they had been friends for years, and then we continued to the other side of the street safely as traffic was at a standstill.

We heard about an incident when a gypsy stabbed someone to death and then fled to his campsite outside town. Gypsies lived on the outskirts of town, not in the city proper. The police went to his home. I suppose he admitted that he committed the criminal act, then he was shot to death by the authorities. That ended that, and no more was said or done afterward. Justice had been served, and the family buried the body. It was a very effective way of policing, which cost the government no more than a bullet. There was no due process, no respect of legal rights, and no lengthy trial.

Living in Spain was like stepping back in time at least twenty years. Our time in Granada was not the easiest for a newly married couple starting out. But we both adjusted, fell into a routine, and made the best of our time there. We met our challenges and were comfortable overall. One thing I did was laundry by hand, including bed sheets. One must become creative and use imagination when there are no laundromats and few homes had washing machines. The real challenge was in the winter, as the bed sheets froze while hanging outside the window on the clothesline, and they were still moist and stiff as a board when they were brought into the house.

Most of the apartments did not have central heating. To our surprise, our first apartment did not have any type of heating. When we rented the first place, the thought never entered our minds about heat, as we assumed there was a heater. It was not until the cold winter set in that we looked for a heating thermostat and discovered none. The sheets were not the only thing that froze: we did also, as the winter temperatures would drop down to freezing. That apartment only lasted until we could find another place nearby Coral's school. The new apartment had central heat; it was not the most effective heating system, but it was better than nothing. At least we had radiators we could snuggle up against during the colder months and that helped to dry our winter laundry on occasion.

In the heat of the summer, for some strange reason, the water would be shut off around 9 in the morning and not come back on till late at night. Perhaps that was why so many people did not bathe more than once weekly. These were the things that made life challenging, but we always managed with a laugh or two. When the water was shut off, it was simply another opportunity for us to become extremely creative. We filled the tub and other vessels with water to enable us to take a bath and clean our apartment. We took what we called a "bucket bath," which was placing a pail of water in the empty tub and washing yourself off using the water from the pail. Hey, whatever it takes to be clean—it worked!

One of the benefits of living in a foreign country was the opportunity to meet people from all over the world. Not only Spaniards, but foreigners from other parts of Europe, the Middle East, Russia, Cuba, Mexico, South America, and many other countries who were there to acquire their education. Some students, of course, were more serious than others. We socialized often, meeting people for meals out or just sitting in the outdoor cafes enjoying a coffee or ice cream.

A number of American western movies were produced in Spain, and we saw the different movie stars walking down the street or at the cafes. The celebrities loved being there, as no one disturbed them for autographs. We saw Chuck Norris and Henry and Shirley Fonda and others who enjoyed the freedom of just being the person next door without the autograph seekers. In fact, one of my good friends Natalie, an American who was married to a Spaniard, Poco, was a tour guide for a number of the celebrities. Natalie had the pleasure of shopping and spending time with Shirley Fonda while Henry was filming.

Strangely enough, most of us low budget students had no telephone but always managed to meet up with friends for outings or gatherings at their home or ours. We met for movies or trips to the Sierra Nevada Ski Resort. Coral did his share of baking apple pies for friends. (Baking was a form of therapy for him.) Overall, we had a pretty nice social life.

Coral was always an early riser, so at first light he was up studying and, afterward, headed off to classes taught exclusively in Spanish. We were both rather fluent fairly soon. He would come home for a brief lunch, return to his studies and classes, then return back home for dinner, and study until he went to bed.

There were no gyms or fitness centers at that time, but Coral, being an avid jogger in the summer heat or winter cold, would jog around the Plaza de Toro bull arena for exercise with our mutt dog, Pepe. Pepe was a gift to me from our janitor. Pepe was such a small puppy, he found comfort in one of Coral's house slippers, where he would curl up and go to sleep. It was funny to watch Pepe as he grew larger and could no longer fit into that slipper no matter how hard he tried. He finally ended up sleeping on and around the slipper, using it like a pillow. I suppose Pepe adopted us, rather than us adopting him.

On Sunday afternoon at cinco de la tarde (5 p.m.), we could hear the roar of the crowd during the bull fights. All we had to do when we attended the bullfights was to just walk across the street to the bull arena.

My time was filled by teaching English and pre-ballet classes to young people. I was fortunate to become involved with a ballet school, which was started by my friend

Natalie who had been a dancer with the Philadelphia Ballet Company, and I even made a few bucks to help increase our limited funds.

Sculpture classes and other art classes kept me busy when I was not out and about with friends. There were endless movies to be seen. Watching movies helped improve my Spanish, and admission was really cheap—only a few pesetas, or about 15 cents. Movie going fit the budget for both of us.

Actually, everything was within our limited resources: even hair salons cost 25 cents for a wash and set in the 1960s. What more could a wife of a poor medical student ask for? I shopped daily for our needs, just like the native Europeans. I bought milk that was not refrigerated; meat and chicken was often on the floor of the meat market rather than hanging from a hook. Many homes did not have refrigerators, another reason for the daily shopping, so food, especially meat that needed to be kept cool, was hung outside their windows.

Going to the market every day was also a way for the housewives to visit with each other. We had a five foot tall refrigerator, so it wasn't necessary to hang our food outside the window. Luckily, we had central heat unlike many of our neighbors and other people in the community. Most people used a bracero for heat—a round dining table with a ledge circling the bottom of the table where your feet were placed and one could find warmth. A heavy wool table cover would be placed on top, forming a lap blanket. When we left the table, the room was freezing and so were we. In a word, *it was cold in the winter*. Often the walls in the apartment would have black mold from the moisture and mildew that accumulated during the winter months. In the summer, however, it disappeared.

After five years living in traditional Spanish culture, Coral graduated at the top of his class and we left Spain in 1972. Coral took the Flex Exam, which was required of all foreign medical graduates. Later, he became one of the examiners for the State of California, overseeing the recent medical school graduates taking that same exam from other foreign universities.

We returned to San Diego because he had been accepted into the residency program at Balboa Naval Hospital. After a short while, he became the chief medical doctor overseeing all the medical dispensaries at Camp Pendleton. While he was doing his residency, I became a real estate agent selling many properties in the San Diego area, both resale and new sales, and met and worked for many of San Diego's leading developers. I continued my education, obtaining my degree in Criminal Justice and later obtained my Juris Doctor Degree from Western State University College of Law in 1983.

A couple of years later, Coral applied for a position at Southern California Permanente Medical Group, better known as Kaiser, to join their staff as an Ophthalmologist. He was accepted on the staff at Kaiser. Coral and Doctor Steve Munz, another Kaiser Ophthalmologist, set up the Ophthalmology Department in Anaheim, CA, in Orange County. Both Coral and Steve became partners at Kaiser, and Coral practiced medicine with Kaiser until his retirement in 2005. For ten years, he also served on the Board of Directors of Southern California Permanente Medical Group, one of the largest HMOs in the United States. Coral was loved by both staff and patients, who long after his retirement inquired about him.

I started working for the Department of Transportation as a Legal Liaison in the Right of Way Department, mainly handling the property acquisition and eminent domain issues associated with property acquisitions along Interstate 5. Often, I would travel between Orange County, Los Angeles, and Sacramento. I thought nothing of flying up to Sacramento and back to Orange County within my regular workday.

We built our home in the early 1990s in the coastal town of Laguna Beach, California, and lived there almost 18 years before moving to the central coast of California when we both retired.

I studied art and became involved in the arts while living in Laguna Beach. The three festivals held there each summer drew thousands of people from all over the world. I successfully showed my art at Art-a-Fair for three or four seasons. I created floor art that sold all over the world. My art could be found at the St. John's Home stores in South Coast Plaza, Palm Springs, and Las Vegas.

We left Orange County and Laguna Beach, which we enjoyed, mainly because of the traffic and congestion, as so many people were drawn to this incredible beach locale with its art and art festivals.

By the time Coral had retired, there were very few places we had not traveled. We had visited over 75 countries. We often traveled with friends or other doctors and their wives from the Kaiser family.

After we retired—I from the State of California in 2000 and Coral from Kaiser in 2005—we relocated to the small community of Cambria, another seaside community, about 45 minutes north of San Luis Obispo along Highway 1. We bought a home with a magnificent white water ocean view from every room in the house. We loved being in Cambria: what a special place, with its natural beauty and some of the most amazing people you would ever want to meet. We were comfortable and happy.

We watched whales from our decks as they migrated past. We enjoyed seeing the deer roaming the area. We were involved in most community events, including the local parade, Community Emergency Responders' Team (CERT), local theatre performances, hiking the many scenic trails with the walking club, and participated in the annual 5.5 mile kayak event from San Simeon to Cambria. Coral also became involved with MOAA, Military Officers Association of America, as their Vice President as he was a retired Navy Commander.

The thrill of a lifetime opened up for me when I was accepted at Hearst Castle as an interpretive guide on the hilltop. The guides at the castle are some of the best trained guides in the country. It was a delight to study and learn about the life of William Randolph Hearst, who started building this monumental structure in 1919. The Hearst

San Simeon State Historical Monument was open to the public after being donated to the State of California in the 1950s by the Hearst Corporation.

In 2013, I wrote a book, *The Saints of San Simeon* (available on Amazon) on the central coast of California dedicated to the saint's devotional art collected from all over the world by William Randolph Hearst.

After leaving Hearst Castle, I became a docent at Mission San Luis Obispo de Tolosa. Nothing delighted me more than providing historical information to the general public. I was a docent at Cambria Historical Society and was involved with the local arts association. For such a small town as Cambria, there are more than an abundance of opportunities to become involved.

Now that you know a little background about us and our lives, which were busy, happy, and very fulfilled, let me move on to what changed that life. Illness destroyed that life style of so many years and led us away from a life we both cherished. We had to say goodbye to all we loved, to our very existence, to our way of life, and to who we were as a couple. Everything was gone in a flash.

My life's journey continued as we stepped out of our world, our life, in an instant. We would only have 48 happy years of marriage together. We would never make that fiftieth golden anniversary celebrating as we had in the past.

CHAPTER TWO

Early Stage Cognitive Impairment

What's wrong with Coral?

MY HUSBAND WAS diagnosed in 2012 with cognitive impairment. I went into a mode of waiting and watching his behavior. We must reckon with the stolen years as that is what this illness does: it steals your life, your past, and your future. I will never forget the first indication something was wrong with Coral. My understanding of this illness was nada (nothing), no comprehension. I wish I had known then what I know now, but I had to learn along the way. But, isn't this life? Isn't this what comes along and derails your plans? This would be new to both of us. We would somehow learn to maneuver through the challenges of dementia in our near future.

The first indication anything was wrong with Coral was while traveling on Interstate 15, returning to Orange

County from San Diego. Coral was driving north to the 91 Freeway. At each freeway exit, he would ask me if this was our exit, and I would tell him, "No, we have much further to go." I do not know why I didn't tell him to pull over and let me drive. After Coral asked me this the entire way home at every exit, I felt frustrated with him. He should have known we would not reach our destination for an hour or so. What was the matter with him? This was not his typical behavior. I had a mixed reaction, as I truly had no idea what to think. It is hard to surmise when things happening are not rational.

When we arrived home, I said, "I am calling your doctor tomorrow so he can see you because something is not right." He proceeded to sit on the sofa in the family room looking exhausted. He just did not look right. For the first time in our lives, the paramedics were called and, after they examined him, they concluded he was having a heart attack. I was floored—I felt as though I was having a heart attack. I could not believe this was happening. Their conclusion could not be right. We had spent a couple of days in San Diego having a relaxing time, with nothing at all stressful about our time there.

The paramedics took him to the local hospital, and, by the time I arrived and was able to see him a couple of hours later, the nurses informed me his heart was as strong as an ox. After he stayed in the hospital a couple of days, he was ready to be released; however, something was not normal about him. I just knew something was wrong in my heart of hearts, but what?

Of course, at this time I only knew the terms dementia or Alzheimer's from medical publications or the news media. Like many other diseases, these are gradual diseases that sneak up on a person. The person with dementia starts to do subtle little things out of character. These actions are not obvious or consistent in the beginning, and may or may not seem strange at the time. It is hard to describe: they are things you cannot put your finger on. It is typical to just live in this situation for a period of time, sometimes for years, before one notices this odd behavior is consistent. By then, the person may well be in the middle or advanced stages of the illness. Dementia would have been worlds away in my thinking, as that illness never even entered my mind. The doctors found nothing wrong with him so could no longer keep him in the hospital.

My intuition led me to take a step further, so I made an appointment with a Neurologist. I felt he merited a visit with another doctor to determine if I could find some answers. I was feeling shock and dismay. It was difficult to comprehend, and I have no idea, even today, why I thought a Neurologist was the type of physician Coral should be seeing. It was like I was being guided by some unknown source. It is difficult to explain and difficult to comprehend. Whatever was wrong with Coral was in his head, not his healthy-looking body.

Later in my research, I discovered that in the early stage, a person may function independently. They may still drive, work, and be part of social activities. This is also when family and friends may begin to notice difficulties, as I had.

During the appointment, his first neurologist gave Coral some kind of simple test, which revealed signs of cognitive impairment. This did not mean much to me at the time—after all, what did I know? The doctor never labeled it further; perhaps that was all it was at that time. The physician never made mention that this could lead to something worse.

He did not tell us this loss of short/long term memory would progress. In order to understand what we were told, I did more research on the web and found cognitive impairment meant a little memory loss and could be progressive. The doctor did say his memory took in new information, but the new information just did not stick in his memory bank. Well, that did not sound too bad, after all. As I said, what did I know? I felt the doctor, Coral's colleague, was being gentle with his information. Perhaps the doctor did not want to give bad news to someone he knew so well. Who knows? I wish his first neurologist had spelled out in more detail what this was and what it could lead to. I wish I had known enough to ask more questions.

If he had said this could lead to Alzheimer's, which is severe intellectual deterioration, or even dementia, which is memory loss, difficulty knowing people, places, time, or season with a loss of ability to make good decisions and loss of safety awareness, my level of understanding of this illness would have placed us in a superior position early on. Perhaps he could have led us to more information, flyers, or even web sites telling us the possibilities that may lay ahead of us. Dementia can lay dormant for many years before it can start to show itself in one's senior years. In Coral's case, he was in his 60s and 70s.

We made numerous trips to southern California doing all kinds of tests, including one that was three hours long, but he passed with flying colors. We were both so glad, and I thought, *this is not so bad and will be okay after all.* But he was a smart guy, and he knew how to take and pass a test. This type of test was one where it is only given in certain specialized locations and we were sent to Hollywood for Coral to be tested. I visited the L.A. County Art Museum until he called for me to pick him up after the test was completed. He informed me he had passed the test. As I reflect back, was he honest with me in telling me he had passed, or had he not told the truth, trying to avoid what may lie ahead?

We celebrated his passing the test by having dinner at *The Sinking Rose* Restaurant in Beverly Hills that evening. Yeah, good news! We also celebrated our forty-fourth wedding anniversary that evening together.

Coral was more comfortable being in Orange County seeing doctors, as the O.C. is where he practiced medicine for so long. He felt at home being seen in a familiar environment with familiar places and faces. This required our driving back and forth from Cambria to the Los Angeles area. Not only was the heavy traffic inconvenient, but also overnight costly hotel stays.

At that time, on the Alzheimer's website, I discovered a list of ten things that very well could be related to these diseases:

- Memory loss that is starting to disrupt daily life.
- Poor judgement and decision-making.
- Misplacing things and being unable to retrace steps to find them.
- Trouble completing everyday tasks.
- Problem solving or planning difficulties.
- Confusion about location, time, date, or season.
- Stepping away from social or work activities.
- Problems with vision and spatial awareness.
- Problem writing or speaking.
- Mood and personality changes.

My curiosity took me to Google in my efforts to confirm my feelings about this diagnosis. I wanted to learn more to give us a chance to seek treatment and plan for the future. At the same time, I did not want to know. However, I read the first five, then slammed the computer shut as I realized he met the first two of the five things on that list. I suppose since I just did not want to know the truth, I didn't want to read the rest. This, I thought, must be the beginnings of this ailment. This was around 2013, and his original diagnosis of cognitive impairment was in 2012.

With a change in attitude, I made up my mind to learn as much about this illness as I could from the web, but also by joining the Alzheimer's Association and Alzheimer's support groups. The group met monthly in Morro Bay, about 20 minutes from our home. I could not bury my head in the sand and hide in a fantasy world. I needed to understand what this horrific illness was so I could be better prepared for the onset.

One of the questions his doctors asked was if Coral had played football. Coral played football in high school, in college, and at the Rams training camp years ago in his youth. The second neurologist did brain imaging and found there were plaques on the brain and signs of past small mini strokes. His behavior, at this point, was still rather normal, with the exception of what had occurred in the car on the freeway. He was still driving as neither Coral nor I knew any better, and at this stage with his doctor visits no one told us it would be better if he was not driving. I did notice he was driving slower and using a lot more caution than what I thought were his normal driving habits. After all, this is a man who had been driving a Porsche sports car for most of his adult life, a typical man who liked to break the speed limit on occasion. (I hope no California Highway Patrolmen are reading this!)

We continued with different medical visits, with nothing much rendering anything that was new or different. The only medication he was taking was just the same general hypertension and cholesterol medications that so many other people take daily. Our life cruised along, as it had in the past years, until early 2015. Our situation was shifting and becoming a little unpredictable and erratic. Coral was still managing to have normal days, still enjoying life, most of the time, though those normal times were starting to become rarer because of the subtle out-of-character behavior I was witnessing.

We began to live the emotional roller coaster that comes with dementia. It was in early- to mid-2015 when I noticed the small things that Coral started to do that were very much out of character. We had, months earlier, planned three trips to Europe in 2015. The first trip was to Holland in the spring on a river boat with a musical group from San Luis Obispo. The second trip scheduled would be to Granada, Spain, for his forty-second medical school class reunion in June. The last and final trip in October was to Greece with friends of ours living in Cambria. Little did I know would these truly be our final travel days? I suppose there may have been a hint this was becoming a reality, but I chose to ignore this.

In hindsight, these trips were so defining. I feel what continued to stimulate Coral's unusual behavior was brought to light because he was taken out of his comfort zone. I could see the difficulty he was having in an unfamiliar circumstance and unfamiliar environment. Whenever we traveled, each of us would pack our own bag asking the opinion of the other person about what would be best to bring on the trip. The trip to Holland was an 18 day riverboat trip in the spring. I was surprised when I noticed Coral had packed 20 pairs of socks, several blazers, multiple underwear bottoms, and no under shirts. As I observed him packing, he would pack then take items out of his bag and then add them back in again. The packing dilemma was stressful for him; he was not asking for help, but I could see he desperately needed me to assist him.

Each time I attempted to correct his packing, he would agree with me that he was a little confused, but when we removed the excess of what he had packed, he managed to put it back into his case again. I made several attempts to help him; however, with each effort on my part he would eventually unpack it or add more of what was already packed. Finally, I sort of gave in as my efforts were not helping him to pack appropriately.

I have heard stories from others in the support groups telling of spouses in the earlier stages having a problem with packing or even dressing by adding more clothes on than usual—often times, even putting clothes on back-ward or just not being able to make a selection in order to get dressed.

Coral was always neat and an easy roommate to travel with, as we each respected the other person's space. In our hotel room, he did something else which was unlike him. He started to rummage in my cosmetic bag looking for his things. When I asked what he was doing, he merely said he was looking for whatever was on his mind. I explained that his things were never in my bag and asked him why he was looking there. Finally, in my lack of understand-ing, I moved all my bathroom items into the bedroom onto the dresser and told him the bathroom was all his. That seemed to eliminate his going through my bag.

There was not much else out of character or out of the ordinary on that trip, except he did stay rather close to me as we roamed the city on foot. Later, as I learned more about this disease, I discovered that a person with dementia stays close to their caregiver as the caregiver becomes a sort of security blanket to them.

Since I became Lonely Planet in human form before and during our trips, Coral, with his agreeable self, always went along with whatever was planned. He would look to me to tell him what we were doing that day and what the itinerary was.

Once we reached our destination, walking allowed us to see sights we could not fully see from a motor coach. We would walk for miles to experience museums, neighborhoods, and feel the pulse of the city. When we visited Amsterdam, we walked along the canals dodging bicycles as they had the right of way. But it was still magical to us.

We stumbled upon the Museum of Handbags near the end of our day walking back from the Van Gogh Museum. Coral was more than agreeable to seeing the museum, but he felt he was a little fatigued from so much walking. He said he would wait in the coffee shop while I perused the displays of purses. After all, a gal could not refuse seeing handbags.

It did not occur to me that Coral may or may not have remembered where he was or might walk off into the unknown world. How horrible I would have felt had I lost him. Looking back, it was not smart to leave him unattended.

Knowledge is power. If I had a complete understanding of this illness, I would have done things much differently. But I too was learning along the way, and everything that was happening was not only new to Coral, but also new to me. In my mind, I was still thinking I could tell him something, as I always had in the past, and he would follow up or be where I asked him to be. At this stage, at least to me, it was mainly confusion, like the packing incident—certainly no concern with him becoming missing. I, too, just did not comprehend the situation. It would take more time for me to understand this illness and the effects it was having on him.

After about 45 minutes of viewing the exhibits, I returned to the coffee shop. Thankfully, he was there chatting with the waiter while enjoying his java. After the visit to the Handbag Museum, we squeezed in one more site, the House of Rembrandt. However, both of us became lost wandering the labyrinth of canals leading back to our hotel, but it was all in fun and we finally made it back on time for the happy hour party with our tour group.

We enjoyed our river boat trip and were able to do some pretty fancy dance moves on the boat in the evenings, as we both adore dancing. From what I remember from the rest of that trip, he was moving a little more slowly in his getting dressed and ready. Perhaps it was because of his inability to make up his mind as to what to wear. Otherwise, all went pretty smoothly.

Life continued on in Cambria, both of us filling our time with our normal activities. Forgetfulness and confusion on his part were gradually starting to become more routine.

Coral had received a telephone call from one of his Granada Medical School colleagues regarding a 41 year class reunion. They phoned him in 2014, which only gave us a two week lead time to travel to Spain. This made it impossible for us to travel that distance on such short notice.

Knowing something was a little off with Coral, and never realizing to what degree, I suggested we go next year in 2015, which would be the 42nd year reunion for sure.

We flew to Malaga, Spain, a couple of days before the actual reunion to meet up with one of his classmates. We had a lovely visit in their home overlooking the city and an evening out on the town in one of Malaga's trendy restaurants. When we were not with them, Coral and I enjoyed visiting the city, museums, and the home of Pablo Picasso. Malaga is the home and birth place of the famous artist. Picasso was born in 1881 and died in 1973. He is buried in the south of France as he spent most of his adult life living in France; yet, he is revered in Spain, and there are house museums and other state museums around the country as a tribute to him.

When we drove from Granada to Malaga we were on a narrow road connecting the two cities passing charming villages with rustic, old, whitewashed homes with flower boxes along the windows. The old gentlemen, long retired from their farming duties, would sit outside their homes waving at passing cars. Somehow or other, I miss those little roads going through villages, giving you a window into the village lifestyle. Traveling on the new super roadways eliminates the verdant high desert landscape which is textured eye candy that excites the senses. Perhaps the lack of beauty traveling on the super toll road did cut our driving time down by at least an hour, but I preferred passing through all the quaint whitewashed villages.

When we lived in Granada, the population was a mere 155,000, but had grown so much that we only recognized the old city and what was nearby. When we lived in Granada, there was just a turn off onto the main street entering the center of town; now there were many freeway exits and many new streets that were unfamiliar to us. When we exited the freeway, we were on the outskirts of the city and it was not until we arrived into the heart of the city that some streets were familiar to us both, or at least to me. Some of the old streets also had new names.

We visited museums and monasteries, and many other medieval sites while in Granada. It is a city brimming over with medieval history dating back hundreds of years. Of course, the thrill of being back was seeing old familiar faces, like our friend Paola who ran the ice cream shop. By the way, the line is always out the door and around the corner as theirs is one of the world's best ice cream.

Paola's father founded the *Helado Italiano* (Italian Ice Cream) which had operated at this location well before we lived in Granada in the 1960s. They would never let Coral pay for ice cream when he stopped by. His daughter Paola still runs the business. We knew the family well while living in Granada and really surprised Paola when we stopped in to visit. Her father left Italy for a better life in Spain and founded the Italian Ice Cream Shop in the 1930s directly across the street from the Royal Chapel of Granada where Queen Isabella and King Ferdinand are buried. This chapel or Grand Cathedral was built in 1505 and is the burial place of the Spanish monarchs of that period. It was so good for us to see the old city.

The reunion itself was amazing: almost everyone recognized Coral, embraced him, and were impressed he had traveled so far for this event after so many years. After over 40 years, it was not easy for anyone to remember faces. The faces were new to both of us. The organizers of the event had enlarged the old class photo of their graduating class of the 1970s so people could point to their photo and identify who they were. Then there would be a burst of laughter and maybe a comment, something like, "Where is your hair?" or "Your hair is all white now?" As I observed Coral, he seemed in a bit of a fog, but a joyous fog, with his inevitable smile and pleasant expression. I could see he was somewhat detached and knew he was not totally comprehending all the events taking place, but he was happy and knew he was a part of something very special. The reunion was so important for him to attend as our lives together started here in this amazing little historic place filled with more history than the whole of the country we were from. In a way, coming back to Granada was like closing the door on those youthful memories. No one could have told me at that time that, within a year, Coral would be in a memory care facility. What a difference a year in time makes when dementia enters your life. He may or may not have recognized his old classmates, but he did recall the classrooms where he had spent many hours being lectured.

I am so glad we made that trip: it was more than special for him and for me, too, to be able to see and feel his delight being back after over 40 years visiting his colleagues. I created a photo album of over one hundred photos of that trip for him to have as a memory for as long as he could remember. I felt, even at that time, perhaps he would not have been able to make that reunion if it were the following year, which proved true.

We had returned to Spain several times since leaving in the 1970s, but not back to Granada and not like this, meeting old friends.

We drove back to Malaga from Granada, stayed a couple of days, and flew out to Paris to spend a few days in the Loire Valley. The landscape was dotted by fourteenth- and fifteenth-century chateaux. It was not hard to imagine life under the reign of a King Louis. These palaces are two hours southwest of Paris and a must see when visiting Paris.

We continued our travels aboard the Eurostar train and stopped in London a few days before boarding the *Queen Mary* ship in South Hampton to make the seven-day crossing to New York City. On board the ship, Coral could never remember our cabin number. I did everything to help him recall the number. I wrote the number down and had him keep it safely in his pocket, but he forgot that the note was there. I pointed out the art on the wall that was near our cabin. That was no help, as his mind was made up the room number was whatever was in his head and I could not persuade him otherwise. Fortunately, the cabin attendant recognized Coral's confusion, and, when he was around, he would point out the correct cabin. Often, I would find Coral in the coffee shop or one of the restaurants. I think back now though it did not occur to me at the time, that perhaps because he could not remember the cabin number it was easier to sit there and wait for me to locate him. In the evenings after dining, we continued to go dancing as we always did on cruise ships. We did cut a cool rug on the dance floor most nights. There were a number of people from the UK on board who did a lot of ballroom dancing. We have always danced free style. We thought their dancing was elegant and controlled, and they thought our style was fun and wanted to try it out.

During the three days visiting New York City, we enjoyed seeing many of the city sites. We stayed together at all times except at the hotel check-in. Our hotel accommodations were not ready when we arrived. By the time we were issued the key to our room, it was near the time for us to go to the theatre to see the performance *Kinky Boots*. In haste, and without thinking on my part, I asked Coral to take the bags to our room while I checked us in.

When I arrived at our room, I found no Coral and no bags. Not knowing where Coral might be, I just rode the elevator stopping at every floor and called for him down the hallway. I finally found him after what seemed like an eternity. He was just standing there looking lost and confused. It was my fault, as I had forgotten his confusion and forgetfulness. As it turned out, he was on other floors looking for our room, as he had forgotten the room number and what floor the room was on.

We finally tossed the bags into our room and then made a beeline to the theatre on foot barely in time to see our matinee performance. I don't know how we made it to the theatre minutes before show time. I suppose it was divine intervention that caused me to book a hotel within steps of the theatre.

It was becoming more and more evident that our travel days were coming to an end. We had one more trip planned and paid for months earlier. Our dearest friends had planned to join us. I was a little hesitant about the trip but felt with friends along we could manage his situation. I did not understand how this illness had progressed and how advanced it has become.

Each passing day, this illness was rendering new challenges that you are unprepared for until they happen. Perhaps there was a slight denial on my part, as I did not always want to see these substantial changes, like other people.

Knowing the actual packing was going to be an issue, I thought of inventing a little game. I put both of our suitcases out. We would match whatever the other put into their bag, item for item. Most of his clothes were hung out for him to choose from. This seemed to work, but then he would tinker with his bag, later adding socks and underwear. When he was not looking, I would pull out items not needed from his suitcase. Then he would unpack his case and put all of the clothes back in the closet. He eventually repacked the case with winter blazers for the summer Mediterranean vacation. It dawned on me that he had packed for a business trip. And that was how he dressed during the entire trip. He wore slacks, button down shirts, and a tie, while the rest of us wore shorts and tees. I threw in a couple of short sleeve shirts in the case but never saw him in any of those. Coral, in his mind, was dressing for work, not a vacation.

We needed a van, and Coral was to chauffeur the six of us from Cambria to LAX Airport in Los Angeles, about four hours away. We picked up everyone except one couple who would be meeting us at the airport, as they were already near the airport visiting their daughter in the area.

As we approached Highway 1, Coral steered the van to turn north rather than south. In fact, we would almost always turn south as Big Sur is to the north of us and there are miles of coast line until you reach Carmel. This was a no brainer and something that we all knew and he should have known to do automatically. Again, I was made aware of how disconnected he must was, and perhaps driving and directions were becoming more of a challenge for him. When we arrived at San Luis Obispo, with much insistence, my friend's husband took control of the wheel and drove the rest of the way. He later mentioned that Coral had been driving a little erratic—fast, then slow, then fast again— which I was unaware of as I was chatting in the rear seat.

During our four-country trip to Greece, Albania, Bulgaria, and Macedonia, each day and evening my husband was the best dressed gentleman wherever we went, always in his dress slacks and dress shirt. He did look great, overdressed and hot and out of place, but exceptionally well groomed. I am sure it was not easy for him, since this was a road trip, and we were staying in different locations every two or three days, depending on our itinerary. Most mornings when I woke up, he was completely dressed and packed, which was fine if we were leaving that day. It did not matter how often I would tell him we would be staying another night.

He continued to shadow me by staying rather close to me during the trip, and I kept an eye on his comings and goings. I was able to go out in the evening to shop with the other gals or use the hotel pool to swim and stretch each evening, and he had no problem waiting in the room until I returned. I just did not comprehend the gravity and did not comprehend the advanced stage of this illness. It never dawned on me he might wander off looking for me. It just never entered my mind at that point. "Why not?" you might be asking. It had not happened yet.

It was not until we were in the final stages of our trip that a couple of incidents occurred that really pin pointed his condition and his level of confusion. After being out all morning touring the city of Sofia, Bulgaria, a few people in our group were retuning back to the hotel on the tour bus for lunch. Coral returned to the hotel with the rest of that group while a few of us stayed in the city center to do some shopping and museum visiting. That seemed safe enough to me, as he was with our tour group. When I returned to the hotel around 4:00 or 5:00 pm, Coral was not resting in the room but was sitting in the lobby with his bags packed waiting patiently for me so we could leave in the afternoon. Our departure day was the following day.

He said he had been anticipating my return the entire afternoon so we could leave that day. He just kept imagining we would be departing, so he always wanted to be ready to go. Something in me was devastated, shocked, and overwhelmed and now, more or less, I was starting to understand the severity of what was happening to him. I think I realized at that time we were both in trouble. I had been warned; the red flags were waving. This was my sucker punch in the gut, my alert to watch more closely. I had been put on notice that his thinking was so diverted and his confusion so extensive, this could surely lead to disaster if I did not keep a very close watch over our situation. I had this feeling in the pit of my stomach, yet I managed a smile and had an explanation for his actions to him.

This illness does not wait; it just keeps on keeping on, moving forward every moment. Coral was not changing physically: he was his same handsome self. Sure, he was a little confused here and there, or so I thought. Otherwise, he was as I had always known him to be, but, inside what a tangled web of thoughts he must have been experiencing. This illness is silent and it moves forward in stealing your mind and memory faster than I was able to imagine. Suddenly, I discovered that all we have can be stolen in broad daylight, and neither one of us was sure what the future would hold.

We checked his bag with the bellman in the lobby, and Coral and I walked along the avenue looking at nothing much. He seemed relaxed, but I was rather in shock. We took some photos of nothing in particular, and it was on this day that I finally started to process how our lives were being altered. We were both entering a maze full of obstacles and potential dangers. I finally understood I needed to be more watchful and step up to the plate and be my husband's guardian and protector. It was no longer adequate to tell him where to meet me or what time to be some place. It finally dawned on me that the situation was extremely serious. He was just not processing that information for more than a moment or two. Wow: I finally was absorbing that it was becoming more serious than I imagined. And believe me, I would make mistakes in the future, as I, too, would forget that he forgets.

When you live with a person for almost 50 years and have a certain level of understanding about each other and certain habits, it is not easy to shift gears into another reality. Or is it that you just do not realize the situation completely? Was I living in denial of his condition?

While we were in the Athens airport to return home from Greece, he mentioned needing to go to the men's room. I pointed out a certain corridor we had already passed, and he headed off in that direction. A couple of moments later, a curtain of panic draped over me. I asked myself, *what if he became confused and turned down the wrong corridor?* I knew I could not abandon the luggage to run to the men's room to find him, if he was even in there.

He could have easily wandered off somewhere else. I could not take all of the luggage with me to go looking for him. I was stuck where I was standing. Little did I know there would be more to come of those panic-like moments.

However, shortly after that experience, and in that same airport, we were walking side by side passing multiple lines of passengers in their prospective airline lines. All of a sudden, there was no Coral: where was he? He was no longer walking along with me. You know how it is: I was casually walking, looking around for where the heck I was supposed to go to catch the flight, and voila! All of a sudden, I was walking all by myself. I retraced my steps in my search for him and found him standing in a line with other passengers. He just separated himself from me and turned to stand in any random line. Wow: another opportunity to get lost in a foreign land! By then, I was thinking, *I need a toddler leash to keep up with him.* Was his orientation so impaired that he could not stay by my side in a crowded environment?

Needless to say, we did arrive home safe and sound without any loss of husband. It was a little close at times, but we did it.

There was no way on earth we could manage another trip. Just the packing dilemma alone was stressful enough. The thought of his wandering off in a state of confusion was too much to bear. Our wonderful experiences together around the world had come to a big fat end. As they say, it was great while it lasted. Up to this point in our lives, we had visited so many countries, done numerous cruises, and enjoyed every single moment of our adventures together as a couple. I am fortunate and blessed to have those memories.

There were warning signs that my beloved husband was sinking in quicksand, and I could do nothing to pull him out.

Our adventures were now limited trips to neurologists' offices and computer screens searching for information. I was aware there were some memory issues, and I was finally grasping just how much confusion was in his head and in his decision making, but I still felt I had a limited concept of this illness. I felt at a disadvantage, and I did not comprehend what I should be doing other than what we were doing. We were making trips to doctors and having various tests done, but I felt mystified how to handle what was going on at home. And still at this point no one had mentioned the word "dementia."

Both Coral and I were aware he was losing his memory. He was a doctor with a higher degree of knowledge but was still duped by the ads and commercials. He was prey to marketers of memory vitamins and pills, wasting countless dollars on miracle cures. We were barely inching closer to a diagnosis and any cure was out of reach.

The second neurologist ordered another brain imaging and an MRI that revealed tangles on the brain and prior mini strokes.

His doctors would draw a diagram of all the contributing health factors: high blood pressure, high cholesterol, high sugar and insulin, the standard American diet and stress. But we were already managing those things fairly well. Still, neither doctor mentioned dementia or Alzheimer's disease, nor that it can happen rapidly. Google helped me learn about brain plaque leading to Alzheimer's disease and that it can build up rapidly. It is not clear what starts the plaque formation process in the first place. Coral did play football in his youth and no doubt took some hits to the head, which we are hearing about on the news lately. Our life continued to be as it had been in the past, with exceptions that creeped into our arena that were off course, but still not a major problem.

CHAPTER THREE

Middle Stage

Coral's Behavior is Just Not Normal

MIDDLE STAGE IS typically the longest stage and can last for many years. As the disease progresses, the person with dementia will require a greater level of care. There can be increased risk of wandering and becoming lost. Symptoms will be noticeable to others.

After being married for so long, believe it or not, we had never had an argument. We would disagree or give one another the cold shoulder, but we never argued. Suddenly, we were getting into these stupid little spats about simple stuff. We would get frustrated with each other over the smallest thing, like his not telling me when someone called or his telling me I had not told him something which I knew I had told him. He would become upset when he could not find items in the house and forget what he was looking for. Items were put away in any random place. He stopped remembering where things were in the house. When I asked him to run down to the garage to get something, he would return with any item rather than what I had asked for. Our kitchen was becoming a nightmare, as nothing was being put back in the right place. I would open a drawer only to find what was *not* supposed to be there, and I would have to hunt in the other drawers and spaces for what I was looking for.

Coral was constantly looking for something or other. When we had appointments or other places to go, we never left the house on time anymore, as he had forgotten something that he needed to go back to search for. I kept thinking of how confused he was, and it appeared like more confusion than memory loss. I did not relate the two issues of memory loss and confusion as one thing but as two separate things.

Leaving the house for a doctor's appointment became a painstaking task. It would have been easier to apply for a travel visa to India than get in the car with keys, jackets, and wallets. It took several trips in and out of the house with the car idling before we could officially leave. Being the dance enthusiasts that we were, our bi-weekly dinner dances were always a highlight for us. He was starting to forget them, but, being a military man, he always took command on the floor as he did troops in the field and led me with grace and pizazz. (I thought that a fun statement.) In other words, he never missed a beat on the dance floor, but I had to remind him the dances were taking place.

He was my amazing, fun-loving dance partner, and I miss our dancing together so much. For a time, it was all right to leave Coral in the company of our dog, Sammy. The small neighborhood was familiar, and the two always found their way back home without incident. If both Coral and Sammy were not home when I arrived, I knew he was walking Sammy. If Sammy was at home alone, tracking Coral down was easy. I would drive the neighborhood looking for his car and remind him to come home to dress for the dinner dance that evening.

His routine of going to San Luis Obispo, about 40 miles from our home, for his Military Officers of America Association (MOAA) monthly meetings was becoming a disaster. He would forget routine events. He would show up on the wrong day and then return home and say the other members forgot as no one was there for the meeting. He blamed the other board members for their forgetfulness, not accepting that his mind was slipping. Post-it notes dotted the walls and mirrors throughout the house. A single calendar was no longer enough to keep dates and events straight.

Coral attending MOAA Meeting in San Luis Obispo

Military Officers of America in San Luis Obispo met twice a month on the first Friday of the month and on Wednesday in the second week. Coral being the Vice President, I wondered what he was actually contributing to the meetings and if anyone noticed his memory issues and his confusion. He had been writing articles for the MOAA newsletter published monthly regarding wellness and healthy living alternatives. Of course, that stopped after a while. Since I noticed he was no longer putting his thoughts together properly and in order, I cannot imagine what he was saying at those meetings. I guess that is something I will never know. After all, I was dealing with enough strange behavior at home, which was becoming more and more erratic and unpredictable.

Coral made an annual trip from Cambria to Morro Bay to have his Porsche smog tested. California has stricter restrictions for such vehicles. When he returned home, he said it was done and showed what appeared to be a cashier's check receipt. He said that was the registration fee and the fellow would be sending all paperwork in to the Department of Motor Vehicles. The registration did not arrive, so after some weeks of waiting, and no registration sticker in the mail, I did some checking and found out he needed to forward the information on to the DMV. This was another act of his confusion.

His home office looked like Hurricane Katrina had hit, though, by the way, it was never in the best of order. He received monthly medical journals and his habit in the past was to read them and keep or toss them, depending on the level of his interest. Months of journals wrapped in the original plastic stood like the Leaning Tower of Pisa. His desk was littered with notes repeating the same thing. I finally filled an entire plastic trash bag from his desk of old mail and notes that had lost their meaning.

Over the past 30 or so years, Coral would open, review, and file our monthly statements from our portfolio retirement investment accounts. These monthly statements were also sitting unopened. It became obvious it was time for me to start reviewing these statements, as there was a lack of oversight of our financial portfolio. I gathered the statements and put them in order and announced that I would review and file them each month. I told him I had no idea what more to do with them, but at least I could review the monthly statements to see if they were operating at a gain or a loss. He was comfortable with my doing this and thanked me for helping him. Interestingly enough, when I asked him how much money had been invested and saved in these accounts over many years, he thought for a while and his answer with his sweet sincere face was, "around $500." My poor husband was so confused about his own personal monetary history, more evidence that he was truly at a loss and his reality had changed substantially from the normal. I checked his checkbook and found he was putting deposits and withdrawals into the same column and could not keep the balance correct.

I was starting to realize the importance of advanced legal and financial planning in order to avoid the difficult consequences of waiting too long. I phoned our attorney and explained our situation, and that now it was time to make the many changes regarding property and finances. This allowed me to start the process of updating and amending our trust. Both Coral and I had power of attorney over each other, but now it was obvious he could no longer have power of attorney over me. I also needed to obtain a durable power of attorney for his health care.

Year after year, Coral meticulously organized receipts to ensure our tax accountant had everything he needed for tax season. In 2013, our accountant announced he could no longer do our taxes. When I asked why, he said he could not deal with Coral, who had few answers and a thousand pieces of paper that were more like a puzzle than information. From this point forward, I met the accountant and took over all the tax preparation. We had a wonderful neighbor and tax preparer who had worked for the IRS and retired from there after 30 years, so I felt extremely confident in his abilities to handle our tax needs. He continued to do our taxes even after we left the area. He was a brilliant tax preparer. He retired after the 2016 tax season. I suppose he could no longer take all of these confused seniors bringing in their paperwork at tax season.

We were still enjoying life with its ups and downs, but changes were taking place almost daily in our home. They were subtle occurrences, or so I thought. I was under the impression I was the only one aware of what was happening and not so much our neighbors. My thinking was just that: this is within our home. Other people need not know what was happening. Not true. My neighbors were well aware. Was I embarrassed? Did I feel this was a private matter? I am not sure what I felt. Up until this time, I thought it was all within our four walls. It was not until the neighbors and others started to mention things Coral was doing that I realized the secret was beyond our four walls.

My hairdresser informed me Coral had come into the salon looking for me one day, thinking I had an appointment. It did not matter that I told him I would be at so and so today, or that I had marked on the board my whereabouts. He would forget and go out to look for me elsewhere. This was *wandering*, but I didn't realize this at the time. I just thought it was his confusion, but finally I learned it had a label: *wandering*. I was beginning to fear the worst, since we lived on the edge of Big Sur: he might leave the salon, located in San Simeon, or anyplace else, and head north on the dark winding roads and be lost or drive off one of the steep cliffs. Even when I left a note on the bathroom mirror or slate board or front door of my whereabouts or what time I would return, he had it in his head where I might be, and he would go looking.

A close friend and neighbor told me how Coral was repeating the same thing so very often. Another neighbor said Coral greeted them while out with the dog and kept telling them the same story over and over again. My neighbor across the street ran over to me when I drove into our driveway one afternoon to ask what was wrong with Coral. Coral had knocked on their door to ask if they knew where I might be. Suddenly, I knew what it felt like to have the secret doors of your private life pried open.

He had no problem walking the dog and returning home, as this had been his routine for years. Of course, this could change anytime. It was just that he was so confused and his information so misplaced, and it was hard for me to truly comprehend this confusion. After all our years together, this was so new for both of us.

Since we had a multi-story home with stairs galore, it was not unusual to have one of us grab something from the upper or lower level for the other person. Once, when I asked him to go down to the garage to collect my handbag from the car, he brought up my water bottle. When he retraced his steps and went back down to the garage again, he brought up the car maintenance manual. I never did obtain my handbag until I went down to the garage myself.

He just could not keep any thought in his head for any length of time. Keep in mind, he was trying his hardest to be normal and not let me or anyone else know his confusion. This is all part of the illness: to be the Great Pretender, the Master of Disguise, as his geriatric doctor had informed me. My husband devoted large amounts of energy avoiding discovery.

I think when you know a person with this illness and have known them for so many years, they look the same, they are the same in your mind, but only on the outside. We cannot see the inside; this is an illness where other people say, "But he looks so healthy so normal, that nothing could be wrong." It is difficult to recognize that your loved one may look the same, but they are not who they once were. My husband was on his way to becoming a mere shell of the person I knew him to be.

This was my life's partner, my team mate. We made decisions together; we bounced ideas off each other. This ability was lost right away. It is one of the first parts of the relationship that is lost for couples. I could no longer turn to him and ask his opinion. One might feel as if perhaps one is reading more into the person's behavior than there is. It is difficult to imagine in the future that I may need to make life decisions for another human, but I now need to make decisions that we both would have made together in the past. It looked as though I was becoming *my husband's keeper.*

He was a person I have always looked up to, who was strong and capable, someone who had always been decisive, making his own decisions all his life, from a kid who grew up in East L.A., the Latino Barrio, into a well-respected doctor. A man who served on the board of directors of a major HMO. A man who was a mentor to future medical students and was revered by the community as an encouraging role model. A man who would not take "no" for an answer but forged ahead to get the best out of what life had to offer. His grades may not have been high enough for the 1960s standards, but he still clawed and worked for his medical degree, having to work side jobs to pay tuition. Nothing came free. He was not born with a silver spoon in his mouth, and he found it necessary to leave the United States to pursue his dreams of becoming a medical doctor. Being a Podiatrist was not reaching for the moon for him, but being a full-fledged medical doctor caring for the human race was what he wanted and what fulfilled that dream. He traveled across the planet to make that dream become a reality. He was one who, like so many other great leaders and persons of accomplishment, exercised perseverance to get to where he wanted to go.

He had taken the words perseverance and persistence beyond their true meaning. Now, to think he could not make a simple decision or do some of the simple tasks life demanded. No, this could not and should not be his and my reality. He was my partner in life, and we were supposed to keep each other company in our senior years and sit by the fire and talk about our past and lament about life and the current changing world around us. Memories are all the aged have. The young have hopes and dreams, while the old hold the remains of them in their hands and wonder what has happened to their lives. These are memories that are lost forever. I could say we have lived our life, if not to the fullest, then at least almost to the brim. We were lucky enough to have seen the four corners of the globe. Now, our lives were slipping into this chaos.

Those memories were being suppressed in his mind, and the past was being stolen away from him little by little, moment by moment, hour by hour, day by day, week by week.

The memories were not suppressed in my mind. I thought of that most incredible day when Coral stood tall and alert with his peers when he was promoted to Commander. He was so outstanding looking in his uniform. His mind was clear, sharp, and capable of making major decisions for himself, his patients, and for us. We had the world in our hands, or so we thought. That was then, and this is now. My knight in shining amour was starting to tarnish as a result of dementia. Grateful for a life well lived together, I bless each of my memories of us together. I cherish every kiss, hug, and dance that was ours alone. No, not this: do not take away his dignity.

The dragon was at our door because this was my new reality, this was his new reality, this was our new reality, and I had to deal with it on a plain of realism of what was best for his life and my life. I was on the road of becoming my husband's keeper.

His exterior was the same lovely, handsome, charming man, but inside was a mass of confusion and forgetfulness that increased with each passing day.

We were entering a new chapter in our lives, and I was beginning to understand what navigating through dementia was becoming for us, as our lives were falling apart one day at a time.

Coral had been asked by the local Rotary Club to give a presentation about his life and accomplishments. Oh, boy, was I ever concerned with what he might say or not say. I could tell he could not organize his notes with what he wanted to say. Before the disease, he was capable of presenting to a large crowd of his peers, and the audience would be captivated. This time, I was more than concerned.

He gave the luncheon presentation, and it was nothing like his prior presentations. He paused a lot, and he repeated things, it dragged on, and he did not highlight the important events and people in his life. He neglected to tell them what he was going to say, and it had a beginning, no middle, and no real end. I felt embarrassed for him. He kept talking about how his sixth grade teacher and his mother had motivated him more. He never got into the meat of his life and how he accomplished all of what he had done in the past because he could not recall the story of his own life. If that does not bring you to tears, I cannot imagine what might. They applauded, but I wondered if it was out of their being polite or whether they actually found substance to enjoy.

There were many other examples of his confused state of mind. Garbage pickup was on Thursday, meaning the trash cans normally went out on Wednesday night. He could no longer remember this, so the trash cans literally went out every night. He would roll them down the driveway, and I would remind him it was not the right day. Sometimes, in my fatigue in this small battle, I would bring them back without saying anything. Other times, he would even roll them out to the street, I would tell him it was not the right evening for them to go out, he would then roll them back into the garage, and within minutes turn around and roll them right back out again to the curb, then tell me I was confusing him. His level of confusion was absolutely mystifying to me. In fact, it was starting to confuse *me*.

I kept telling my friends he was okay, as that is what I led myself to think: it was just he was so very confused. It seemed that he was doing things the opposite of what he needed to do. If you said go left, he would go right. He was so confused, but physically he was happy and healthy.

Within my normal mind, if you can call it that, I was attempting to justify his actions as being near to normal, if not normal.

A couple of incidents occurred on the road. Once, he turned into traffic going the wrong direction and, by the grace of God, there was no other oncoming traffic, so we were safe that time. If he made a mistake, he would say I told him to do it; it was common for him to blame me.

Generally, in the morning, we both would go to our separate gyms. Often, as I was driving back home, his car would pass me heading up the hill and I could see he was wearing his white dress shirt, part of his military uniform, and I knew he was heading for one of his non-existent meetings, again on the wrong day. This meant he was driving 45 minutes each way to San Luis only to discover no one was there but him. He would return a couple of hours later very disappointed that he was the only one who showed up. It was getting to the point that no white board alert, no post-it notes on the bathroom mirror, and nothing I could say would change his mind that there was no meeting that day.

One day, both Coral and I were supposed to meet someone for lunch in town, but each of us at two different restaurants just a half block away from each other. I drove us into the village and sat with him until his friend came, but his friend must have been running late, so I left for my lunch. I told Coral to walk down the street after his lunch, or, if I finished first, I would walk to where he was. He agreed with no problem, as the two different restaurants were just a few feet away from each other on the same side of the block.

After my lunch, I walked over to where I left Coral, but he had already left the restaurant. Later, I found out his friend had never shown up, no doubt because the meeting time and date were wrong. Since Coral was not at the restaurant, I headed home. He was not there when I arrived but showed up a little later. When I inquired what happened, he said his friend did not show up, so he walked home. Coral ended up walking up a narrow hill of a road, crossing Highway 1, and then walking on the shoulder of a busy street where there were no sidewalks. Normally, when we walked to the village, it would be along the beach bluffs on the ranchland where there is only foot traffic. But, remember, I said "normally." By the way, he could not recall the name of the friend he was to meet. This was becoming dangerous for him as he was in the path of traffic and crossed a major highway in his efforts to return home. He had a phone to call me, but apparently forgot how to use the phone or that he even had the phone. On the bright side, he remembered where home was and arrived safely.

With all of this going on and visiting his neurologist located several hours away and trying to put all of this in perspective and talking to friends about what was happening in our lives, I was not sure what to do next. I just stayed in my waiting and watching mode. My husband was entering a new chapter in which he would completely lose his sense of himself, and I would lose him. The person I had known most of my life was dissolving and fading away from me right before my eyes.

He, too, knew something was wrong and had an idea his memory was at stake. There are no direct or definitive answers to this type of illness, as each case is different. I heard about the gizmo Phone Watch offered by Verizon. It was typically used for kids, so their parents could keep track of them. The beauty of the phone-watch is there are only two buttons: on and off. He could press the green light to answer the phone, and he could press another button to call me, as it appeared the regular phone had too many buttons and that was too confusing for him to continue to use. This allowed me to feel a lot more comfortable when we were out together or when I was away from home, and it was much easier for us to be able to communicate easily. I did not like leaving Coral for more than a few minutes. Anytime I left the house, I began phoning him often, as well as rushing back home.

Something in your gut sort of tells you to get back home. Although things were more normal at that time than they became later, that everlasting feeling of rushing back home to him was always with me.

You are constantly waiting and watching.

This is a progressive illness and does not revert, nor does it get better. It is a tough illness for both the person who it is happening to and for the care people surrounding the person with dementia. You can only listen to others and hear how they may be handling their situation. I truly met wonderful people telling their story along this part of the journey. Some were doing what I knew I could not do, and others were just doing their very best under the circumstances, and others were dealing with this illness even from long distance.

There are no two stories that are the same, as every person with this illness is different, every situation is unique, and every caregiver is different. There is no timeframe, no looking at the clock and saying, *this will end on a certain day or time*, as there is no way of telling what will occur today or what this odd behavior will bring in the future. It is so foreign to you; that you just do not know what it will bring over the next minute. You are hanging by a thread, dangling in mid-air looking for answers that will never come, as it is one day at a time. There is no time peace; there is no calendar lining up the events to come. You just take what comes at you at that moment. It is truly the unknown.

You are constantly waiting and watching.

The doctor gives you a diagnosis, and you go home, and you live out the nightmare, and it is not easy. You are alone in this, and there is no magic wand. It is up to you to figure out the next path that you are going to take, how you are going to walk the walk in the future.

Whatever decision you make for your future and the future for both of you is *the right one.* If you elect in-home care, or if you decide on a memory care facility for your loved one where you know they are safe and well cared for, that is your decision and your decision alone. You must preserve your own sanity, as this is a road that may be less traveled by many of your friends; they are living a normal life. They do not know your circumstances and can only second guess.

Remember the old sayings, *Walk the walk and talk the talk* and *they are not in your shoes?* You have to make those decisions that will support both you and your loved one. I have heard many stories and I do not judge anyone's choice or decision.

Walking into a support group takes courage your first time. Everything is discussed in confidence. It is okay to cry and to laugh, as this is a sensitive and supportive environment. Each person is unique, and there is no right or wrong. The group comes together to exchange their own personal experience and techniques, trials and errors, successes and mishaps, which might be helpful to others. It is okay to share or not share your feelings and experiences. No one is required to talk, and when someone speaks, they all listen.

In one of the support group meetings, I heard of a woman who placed her spouse of many years in a memory care facility and never once went to visit him—not once—but that was her choice. Perhaps she could not bear witnessing the changes her husband was incurring. It may have been her heart was so broken she could not offer comfort. We will not ever know the reason, but remember she had her reasons. Or, maybe it was self-preservation.

After Coral went into a memory care facility, I always put on my happy face. Not everyone can do this. It's not easy. I always brought him a gift, a small token that would provide him joy. Even if it was just a bag of M&M's, it was something he liked and made him smile. Later, of course, I discovered how hard it is to witness your loved one lost like this illness makes them. As they lose themselves, you are also losing them. Every time you see them, another part of them has vanished.

All the information I was receiving from Coral's doctors did little to help our home dilemma. The doctors talked about plaque. They pointed out images of mini strokes. But I had no idea what to do with this information or how it would change our home life. I found out more about plaque forming on the brain; it is similar to tangles of yarn. It grows and expands. But where was the psychological help? Where was the information to help me cope with daily life?

When would I know when it was time to move in a different direction? How would I know if I could not handle this anymore? What would life be like when I lost my right arm, my buddy, my partner?

Every answer was the same: you will know; you will just know when that time comes. Waiting and watching.

A new world of dark, unknown, and unfamiliar circumstances was on the launching pad. I was starting to live day to day adjusting from having a brilliant self-sufficient husband to undertaking shepherding, coaxing, cajoling, and some trickery. All the while, I was listening to the same story being told over and over.

Dementia is an unrelenting illness. It changes everything.

It steals your life. It robs you of who you are and who you will become.

It robs others, too, as your loss of you becomes their loss of you as well. My questions have no answers, but I continued asking anyway.

What would happen next?

Why and how did this happen to us?

How had my life changed so radically, and why?

Was I a widow even though my husband was still alive?

When did this start? Why did I not see this coming?

How should I have dealt with this onset illness? How could I continue to cope?

How would I redefine myself?

When would it end? Was there no end in sight?

This illness has claimed one victim and I do not want it to claim another—*me.*

CHAPTER FOUR

Hallucinations and Delusions

CORAL'S THIRD NEUROLOGIST prescribed a medication that promised to help him rest and function more normally. It had just the opposite effect.

Hallucinations and *sleep disturbances* are common in the later stages of Alzheimer's disease.

Coral first took this tiny little pill on Monday. A few mornings later, I woke up with him standing at our bed side with an unloaded rifle in one hand and a large souvenir knife in the other hand. I cannot express to you how that frightened me. I was terrified. It was beyond fear and panic. I was speechless. After being married to this gentle-mannered man for almost 50 years, waking up to this was unbelievable.

Once I was over the shock, I asked, "What are you doing?" His answer was that he was protecting us as there was someone in the house. I believe every defense I have ever had fell apart. Not only was I speechless, I was devastated. I just could not believe what was happening. After I crawled out from under the covers shaking with fear, all I wanted to do was hide under them. I proceeded to locate the bullets. If he was going to carry a gun around the house protecting us there would be no bullets available. Could he mistake me for the prowler in our home?

A dark house can be intimidating at night, so I proceeded to install night lights in every room. The rooms must have been dark and possibly haunting to Coral. Our Labrador, Sammy, would bark in the event of anyone coming into the house.

One night, when we were sitting in the living room, Coral looked up into the loft area overlooking the living room on the second floor and was positive there was someone standing there looking back at him. Once again, there was no way I could persuade him that no one was present. It must have been some type of reflection that caught his eye. I went to investigate the spot where he said the phantom person was, but there was no one there.

My nights were frantic now and not my own, as Coral would be restless and wandering around the house. If he woke, I woke, and he woke often during the night. Every time he went to the bathroom, I would wake up and wait for him to return to make sure he was not roaming the house looking for a phantom intruder. Given the sleepless nights and the emotional turmoil, it was a wonder either of us could survive the next day's activities without falling asleep on our feet. Our bedroom had a second room, which was a retreat area. Sometimes, he would return from wandering around the house and just walk in the retreat area, walking in circles with his head down, looking from side to side. That was so painful to observe, my normal friend and partner behaving so abnormally. I could do nothing to help him. I felt so very helpless.

He would insist there was a lion under the bed or there was a homeless person in the corner of the room. Almost every morning, he would be up before me, not reading the newspaper and sipping his coffee, but in search of someone or something in our home. A good night's sleep for both of us was out of the question and had come to an end.

I was exhausted while maintaining much of my normal routine during the day. Every bone and fiber of my body was falling into this state of exhaustion.

I continued with my regular activities. He spent most of his time during the day watching TV, sleeping, and walking the poor dog five to six times per day. Once, I noticed he had been watching the same infomercial over and over.

Sometimes, he would return after walking the dog and 30 minutes later take the dog out again. Again, there was nothing I could say. If I said, "You just came back with the dog," he simply replied that he needed to take him out again as walks were good.

Our dog Sammy standing with his new roommate

Coral stopped going to the gym and continued sleeping off and on during the day. He would sleep in late during the day as he had prowled the house all night.

We continued attending church on Sunday and our every other Wednesday night dinner dances meeting up with our friends. They were aware of what was happening in our lives. My very animated, talkative husband was silent and not participating in any of the conversations as he had in the past. He still had his great dance moves, but his conversations were minimal.

One night around midnight, he sincerely believed someone was in the house. I was at my wit's end and felt so helpless that I ended up calling the 24-hour Alzheimer's helpline to ask what to do. They said to call 911 but ask for an Emergency Medical Technician (EMT) not the police.

Our dog, Sammy, was resting in his bed, which was a fairly good indicator there was no threat. But, in Coral's mind, we were possibly under the siege of a prowler.

I looked down the street and saw headlights heading down the hill. The headlights went out and the car parked several houses away, then the police officers walked onto our driveway. I opened the front door. They asked me to come outside. I explained my husband had dementia and he thought someone was in the house. They asked Coral to come out, which he did; however, he was carrying a large souvenir sword in his hand. The officer asked him to put down the weapon: "Sir, drop the weapon." Coral complied and came down the stairs with both hands in the air.

It was another unbelievable moment that I would not ever forget: seeing my sweet-mannered, kind, very law-observing husband descend the stairs with his hands in the air. He was no criminal. Believe it or not, it was *humorous*, and, as I reflect on that moment, I always laugh. As ridiculous as it sounds, that moment was laughable.

The three officers probably knew him or at least had seen him coming and going around town over the years. We attended different fundraisers in town, one of them being "Tip a Cop," where the different officers serve as waiters and you tip them. Perhaps they knew him from that event.

They searched the house and the backyard and of course found nothing and no one. They inquired if there were other weapons in the house, and I told them yes and gladly gave them the rifle and all the souvenir knives from our many travels. These items would be tagged, logged, and stored at the station until I was ready to pick them up.

After all the excitement and after the officers had left, we were alone just the three of us: Coral, and Sammy, and I. I asked if he felt assured there was no prowler, and he said, "No, there is someone here."

I guess that did it for me. I knew this was reaching a point where there would be no way on God's earth I could continue to handle life as it was becoming.

It was the end of the week that Coral had started taking those pills his doctor prescribed. I called the doctor's office that Friday morning to let him know what had occurred over the week. He said, "Don't allow him to take any more of those pills." He informed me there were other drugs that may be effective; but the side effect could be fatal. Really, now! Are you kidding me? What the hell? Are drugs designed to cure the problem, but then kill the patient? Give me a break. I had seen enough of pill taking.

I spoke with the doctor about my anxiety to leave my home overnight, as I had concerns leaving Coral alone. However, I did not feel safe under the circumstances. I did not want to leave Coral alone all night and at the same time did not want to be there alone with him. Both the doctor and I were in a dilemma, but I made the decision to leave for safety's sake.

That night, out of plain old fear and anticipation of what might happen again, I slept around the corner at my friend and neighbor Maryann's house. Coral called me around midnight to say goodnight and then again around 6:00 in the morning. He had been okay alone, but I felt 10 times better being out of my own haunted house. My home was no longer my hideaway or my sanctuary. It was becoming a place where I did not want to be.

People had told me, when the time comes you will know when it is time to make a change in your situation. I felt I had reached that point. I created every possible excuse to postpone the inevitable, knowing there was no definitive test. No pill, no cure, no way of diagnosing the disease for the better as this illness progressed.

I was not going to live like this anymore. I was afraid. I felt in danger for myself and for him. He was in danger with the decisions he was making. It had reached a point for both of us. It is hard to give support to another when you yourself are falling apart.

Thomas A Kempis said, "First keep peace within yourself, then you can also bring peace to others." I had no peace to give.

CHAPTER FIVE

Moving From Our Home

This Is More Than I Can Handle

IT WAS TIME to make a move. Staying in one's home sometimes is not an option. It was not for me. But how, and when, to make these changes? I was not sure.

One of the things that helped encourage this decision was that, earlier in our marriage, Coral and I had discussed that as we grew older, we would watch each other to see how the other one might be declining. We both agreed that if the other person became incapacitated, we of course would do the absolute very best for that partner but continue living our lives. I reflected back on the past and thought about that conversation. I wanted to do the best for Coral, and I certainly did not want to act with selfish motivations. He was reaching a place where he could no longer function independently without help. He was making poor decisions, and his confusion and forgetfulness were not allowing him to complete the simplest of tasks. It was just one of those crazy things that we had talked about a long time ago as we both looked to our future, without a crystal ball.

Mourn what you've lost; celebrate what remains. Change can feel like a loss, and loss must be grieved before we can fully move on. Part of the process is taking stock of and appreciating what we still have. This was a painful moment in our lives as we were living through hell. The good news was that I realized the changes would be taking place and it was up to me to take stock of what I needed to do and do it. However, at the same time, I realized if I wanted to keep on living my life alone, I had to make positive choices for myself.

The descent towards helplessness is uneven and unpredictable: you think you're on a straight road towards a known destination, but it turns out to be a narrow path winding its way along a cliff edge, full of pitfalls, zigzags, vertiginous views. There often comes a day when something that was being managed becomes unmanaged and unmanageable. How much should one give? Everything? One's whole self? It's always too much; it's never enough.

Several years prior, we had visited Independent Senior Living Communities and liked what we saw and truly thought that lifestyle would be perfect for us when the time came to downsize from our home. We liked the idea of living in a place where every meal, amenity, and transportation would be provided. We thought that was a way to retire as we both aged, which required a lot less work in maintaining one's comfortable lifestyle. We had visited Carlsbad by the Sea Retirement Community years ago and liked their home environment. We placed our names on the wait list with a deposit. Being on the wait list meant they would continue to inform us of what was available as residents moved out. In reality, they knew we would not be ready for such a move for several years.

We told them not to call us for at least ten years. We had even selected the unit configuration that would accommodate our needs so when one became available they would keep us informed and inquire as to our readiness.

We both loved the ocean and this location put us right at the shore. There were so many activities, such as a biking club, a kayaking club, etc. Plus, the location was within walking distance to the shops and restaurants. In other words, it appeared to be a good fit for the future, or so we thought. To make a long story short, as wonderful as all of this pre-planning was, as well as this having been the best laid plan for our future, there was no memory care facility there, so after being on their list for several years, I had to request our wait list deposit back, which they returned immediately.

That is life! The best thought-out plan can change in a minute, and, in our case, it did. After many months of visiting more than one neurologist, it was not until our appointment with Coral's geriatric specialist doctor, who very honestly confirmed my worst fears. This incredible woman laid the facts out for me. She invited me into her office and explained all of this away from Coral, who was in another waiting room.

She informed me that Coral did not have a clue about anything. He was a master of disguise in his effort to be normal. He appeared the same on the outside but was merely a shell of the man he once was. She said it may be necessary to have someone with him when he left home. He was now living in a fog. He did not even know where he was most of the time.

A decision had to be made and fairly soon. Coral was now really having difficulty processing information, to a point he was unable to function normally. His behavior fit the signs of someone with a neurodegenerative condition. She informed me that this was a progressive disease which would only get worse. *Emotionally, spiritually, and physically*, the disease is ruinous, especially for any immediate family. In some ways, it is more difficult for the family because, at a certain point, the actual person who suffers this illness could not care less what is happening, but the caregiver is in constant anguish and stress. Also, a great number of caregivers die prior to the patient, as it takes a tremendous toll on them and everyone involved. Their stress levels are always extremely high, which can lead to other physical symptoms. The disease takes over and eventually leaves the person as a semi-permeable shell capable of recalling only dislodged, random fragments of memory to hold on to. For a spouse, there is just the shell of the person you love, staring out into space.

I was trying to understand the unrelenting chaos and pain this illness can cause.

Coral's doctor reaffirmed the truth. I had been living with this illness and knew it would only become worse with time. I could see the writing on the wall. There was nothing but time in the future, and I did not like what I could foresee. I did not like what was happening to Coral, and I did not like what was happening to me. The stress and strain of all this was as unrelenting as the disease. The pressure, tension, worry, frustration and conflict in our home was becoming too much to bear.

In January 2016, after getting the final doctor's recommendation of his decline, I asked the doctor, "What would you do under these circumstances? Would you make a drastic move into more secured assisted living?" Her answer was, yes, she would. I cannot tell you how much I appreciated her telling me the truth and not skirting around the issue.

Her honest approach allowed me to make the best decision and move forward with what I thought was better for both of us because I had no view into his world, nor did I have a crystal ball or map guiding me. I was on my own, so here we come world. He continued to follow me to the driver's side of the car rather than the passenger's side; he was always right behind me; and if I turned around I would literally run into him. It was actually becoming a little uncomfortable.

Coral was no longer driving as his third and last neurologist had informed us California law required him to send the Department of Motor Vehicles notice regarding

Coral's diagnosis and the possibility of their revoking his driver's license.

The Department of Motor Vehicles sent him forms to fill out in the event he wanted to come in and take the written and driver's test. Coral mentioned they were trying to take away his license and preventing him from driving. Those forms sat on his desk for weeks. I knew I was not going to aid him in filling them out, nor was I going to drive him to the DMV, because he should not have been driving, as I feared for his safety and the safety of others. I had already hidden his car keys from him. He misplaced so many things, it was easy when he asked if I had seen his keys to say I had not. He really did not push the issue much anyway. You cannot imagine the anguish I suffered about stopping his driving. I was grateful the doctor and the State of California removed that responsibility and burden from my shoulders.

I speak to caregivers today who find it such a challenge stopping the person they are caring for from driving. When a doctor makes the recommendation, often the caregiver is limited to hiding the keys, or fixing the car so that it won't run. Eventually the person suffering from dementia might just forget about the car, while others can be very persistent.

Hope has two beautiful daughters, Anger and Courage. Anger at the way things are, and courage to see that they do not remain as they are.

— Saint Augustine

We were launching on the biggest adventure of our lives, but this adventure would take us onto two separate paths. It was time to look to the future to determine the best solution for us. However, I was in limbo. I was angry at this disease for what it was doing to someone I cared so much about. But, drawing on my faith, and the words of Saint Augustine, I felt with courage and perseverance, I could face the future and make the best decisions with a positive frame of mind. I truly believe, as we travel through life, we choose to make any mission either positive or negative. Making up our mind about what to do is the greatest challenge. But, once we do make a decision, moving forward isn't as hard as we had envisioned.

With the advice from the doctor, leaving her office I felt comfortable going directly to one of the senior retirement communities we had visited in the past and we both liked.

Why there and not at home? It felt better to be in a place where Coral might be familiar, at this stage in his transition, meaning an easier transition into memory care for him later. I wanted him to have as much peace of mind as possible. That location allowed him the ability, when the time came to go into memory care, to adjust better than leaving our home and going directly into memory care. I would be living just across the courtyard from where he would be living. I thought this the very best plan and place for both of us at that time. His doctors were in Ventura, and we needed to be near to them.

We rented a one bedroom apartment, month to month, with a balcony overlooking some lovely trees blowing in the breeze. It was around 700 square feet, and I felt it was right for our new lifestyle. I wrote the check for the first month's rent and a community fee—a fee is generally required by the majority of retirement communities—and gave them a potential move-in date.

I had considered perhaps leasing a one-story home in Ventura and moving lock stock and barrel from our Cambria home. That would have been such a major mistake, as I would have been saddled with a home full of our belongings and living alone as his condition greatly changed with each passing month. That would have been like trading tit for tat, not a practical move. Perhaps I was acting on a leap of faith, but, in the end, that decision was the best for both of us. Thank God, the man above was in my corner and helping me plan our dubious future.

We drove back to Cambria and that is when I started packing boxes and placing them in the retreat area of our bedroom so we would not have boxes all over the house and our home would not look like a moving and storage warehouse.

After all, we were moving from a rather large home to a small apartment. I needed just the basic furniture and other things that fit into the space, enough to be comfortable. This was going to be the first of many moves clearing out of our home. Coral and I went out shopping for a new bed to be delivered the day of our arrival to Ventura. I knew what I was attempting to accomplish; however, I had no idea what Coral was thinking about this shopping adventure looking for a new bed—after all, our bed was just fine.

My packing consisted of a couple of comfortable chairs and a breakfront to house our TV, a couple of lamps, and a few other pieces I held near and dear to my heart to add warmth to the new location. Coral never asked about my packing: perhaps in his state of mind he thought I was spring cleaning. With all of the changes happening within our home, he had a non-curious detachment. We talked about the move, and he was aware the movers would be arriving with a truck to haul off the packed boxes. He just seemed disconnected from what was going on. By then, he was sleeping less at night and sleeping on and off during most of the day when I wasn't home.

He was restless but in good spirits otherwise. His behavior improved for the better, being taken off the anti-psychotic drugs. Fortunately, getting off that medication removed most of those delusions. But the effects of those medications needed to clear out of his system before he would return to his more normal self. He should never have been placed on those types of drugs.

Later, I learned these drugs are increasingly being used for management of non-psychotic disorders. They are a major tranquilizer for management of schizophrenia and bipolar disorder, not dementia. One acting as a caregiver really needs to talk to the attending physician to make sure they know the medications their loved one is being given, as well as the side effects when taking these drugs.

However, like so much else about this illness that, too, was on the job training.

One evening, I truly thought I was having a heart attack, as my chest would not stop pounding. I mentioned this to Coral, and we both agreed the paramedics should be called. The paramedics arrived to find my blood pressure was over 200; I have never had a blood pressure issue. They recommended rushing me to the hospital in San Luis Obispo, about 40 miles from our home. My concern was that I did not want the paramedics to take me there because Coral would get into the car and follow, and he was not supposed to be driving. If the paramedics left, then how would I get to the hospital? Luckily, our wonderful neighbors next door, Julie and David, saw the paramedic's van in front of our house and came over. They ended up driving us to the hospital in the pouring rain. My concern was also their concern about Coral driving. At some point, the paramedics must have been wondering why they could not take me to the hospital. Julie and I were on the same page regarding not letting Coral even think about getting into the car to drive.

This tiny, sweet community of very caring people was one of the many reasons we did not want to leave and live any place else. This is the care and concern that is in the sweet little town of Cambria. We arrived at the hospital around 11:00 pm. However, I was released early the following morning around 2:00 am. As it turned out, I was not having a heart attack; I was simply stressed to the maximum. I am only telling you this so you realize the stress the caregiver can have, which may or may not result in a health crisis. In other words, this was starting to take a toll on me not only emotionally but physically. These physical problems are real. It is estimated that seventy-five percent of routine visits to doctors are stress related. One of the greatest causes of stress is caring for a sick loved one. A broken heart takes a toll on the rest of your body. There was not much I could have done to reduce stress in our home. I truly believe, had we stayed in our home with me acting as his caregiver, I would have eventually lost it all together. In many ways, caregivers are at a greater risk than the person they are caring for. They, too, can become like a shell of their former self.

My fear of the truth finally became a reality. It was not merely his being forgetful and confused; it was more than that. This illness was on its way to changing our lives in ways I never dreamed possible, slowly but surely.

Coral had started displaying even more memory lapses, odd behavior, mass confusion, and inability to do a simple task in his daily life. I was becoming my husband's keeper as he was becoming "undone" due to dementia.

When he got something into his head, no matter what he was told, it was impossible to convince him otherwise. His inability to accept anything other than his own reality made caring for him impossible. His reality and my reality and that of the rest of the world were at odds. I feared for his safety and was concerned that he might disappear as various stages of decline started to take place.

My delaying and denying our coming day of reckoning with this illness would only increase my anxiety as time passed.

It was important to me that, when this illness rendered him in a condition that was more than I could manage alone, even with professional help, that he would be in a safe, familiar environment and I would be close by. I knew very little about this or any other illness. I was fearful of what might come next and felt I had no one to turn to for help. Relocating to senior community housing allowed us both some level of security. That was my thinking in the beginning of my leap of faith into our new future.

There was no doubt in my mind that the big, bad, really ugly *dragon* was at our door. It was time to begin the process of relocating from our home.

We had lived in Cambria over 10 years, and our plans were to stay for years to come. This was our retirement home; this was where we both wanted to be. We were aware in years to come that we would leave Cambria and the two of us would go into a senior retirement living arrangement. It was just that neither of us thought it would be then, but much later. Plans do change, don't they?

I had seen the stress of what some of our friends and neighbors had gone through with similar illnesses. I did not want to walk down that unpredictable road in our home alone.

CHAPTER SIX

Taking Some of the Stress Off-Relocating to Senior Independent Living

EARLY THE NEXT morning, Coral and I finally left our comfortable home in Cambria. The day before, Meathead Movers had packed the truck with the furniture for the apartment and would be meeting us in Ventura the following day when we drove down. As Coral's diagnosis of dementia progressed, we would remain there, since it had the convenience of being near his doctors. This felt much better than being in our home because there were no more long drives to the doctor, no more of his being haunted thinking someone was hiding in our home. No more of my calling for help in the middle of the night because of his hallucinations. His doctor made it clear why he stayed so close to me when we were away from home: I was his security blanket. Dementia patients need to have someone near them who they feel they can trust. That person was me, and I was in it for the long haul.

Evenings were always quiet, as residents would tuck themselves in their suites by 7:00 pm. A sense of loneliness was pervasive. Residents were eager to meet someone new. It was called an active senior community; however, it appeared to be more of an independent *slightly* active community. Some residents drove, but most did not, or should I say, should have not.

Coral was in his mid-seventies. The average age of most seniors in retirement communities seems to be in the eighties and nineties. It was an entire community of elderly people, with the exception of a couple of folks who were younger, at least in spirit, if not in age. The residents were warm and friendly, and we found them to be immensely funny and enjoyable. Of course, we had been around older people, but never surrounded and emerged in an elderly environment such as we were then. My thoughts were that Coral must have been struggling, as even I was attempting to remember the names of the many residents we shared the community with. I am sure he did not remember their names, but he always greeted each new person with his same sweet smile.

When we first relocated to Ventura, Coral thought we were in Las Vegas. We had driven to Ventura multiple times to visit with his doctors; but, in his mind, we were in Las Vegas. He accepted our one bedroom apartment as being a hotel room, although our apartment was filled with our furniture and things I thought were familiar to him. He did not quite comprehend having the furniture movers place our belongings in this apartment or that it was more than just a hotel room.

In the beginning, he would ask, "When are we going home?" My reply remained the exact same words each time he would ask: "When your doctors think it is time will be when we return home," which he accepted as fact; he seemed to feel comfortable with that same answer each time he asked.

After a few weeks in Ventura, he stopped asking about going home and seemed to have accepted this new place as being our home. Shortly after we relocated into senior housing, he commented it was like being on a ship that did not leave the port, which I thought was good reasoning on his part. My answer about returning home seemed to be giving him comfort. This same answer was as per the recommendations from the support group from the Alzheimer's Organization. I was told it is easier to relocate a person with dementia earlier than when the illness is in its later stages.

He especially enjoyed the dining experience more than anything else, as it appeared his appetite had increased. He never missed the three meals prepared daily. Often, he ate two lunches and was always ready for dinner. The menu was varied, and it was nice how they set up plates daily by the entry to the dining room, so you could see exactly what was being served. It is true what they say: *A picture is worth a thousand words.* The display made it much easier for Coral to make a meal selection.

My most important concern was that he appeared comfortable there as things were becoming familiar to him. We would walk the neighborhood going to the coffee or yogurt shop. We explored the area on foot looking for the different neighborhood parks. We always went together, of course, and he seemed to be adjusting just fine. He would every so often ask again when we might go back home, and my answer was always the same: "When your doctors say it is time," and he continued to accept this without further question.

Remember to follow the rules; it makes life a lot more reasonable for both of you. Whatever the person with dementia says, you always agree with them. Their reality and your reality are two different things. There is a time to be honest, but, under these circumstances, there is a time to use what the Alzheimer's Organization calls fib-lets.

The first couple of weeks here, I was able to go to the YMCA for my gym classes in the morning for about an hour. Coral would go down to the dining room for his breakfast and returned to our apartment unit alone. Occasionally, he forgot how to get back to our apartment unit and would find himself on another floor or perhaps wander into the other building on the site looking for our apartment, but it did not seem to be a concern as he never left either building. His confusion persisted, but staff, in their gentle nature, would redirect him to the right place. Once back in the apartment, he would turn on the TV and be watching his favorite show until my return. I was finding senior living took a great deal of the pressure off me.

His ability to be slightly independent only lasted for a few weeks, then I gave up going to my morning exercise classes as I was concerned leaving him alone. After a while, I learned about care service agencies from which I could hire a person to sit with him until my return that way he would never be by himself. His confusion continued to become worse. There were times I would observe him opening the closet door when he wanted to go to the bathroom, or go into the bathroom when he should be looking in the closet. Poor Coral could not master one single task and was doing the opposite of what he should have been doing. He also showed a great deal more fatigue than normal.

After each doctor's appointment we learned a little more about his memory issues, but he was not getting any better.

Sometimes, he would wake up in the morning and say that we were packing up that day and leaving. In the middle of the night, he might leave the bedroom and go into the living room and sleep in the chair. I felt every day was a new challenge, and I was constantly putting out fires. I adjusted to Coral's behavior as best I could, and often I was at my wit's end. I had little quality of life and felt trapped by his dementia. Even with all of these adjustments, living there was working out better than at our home. He was not thinking someone was hiding in the corner or under the bed anymore.

I had no idea how long we would be living under those circumstances. We had just left our home and disappeared from Cambria before most people even knew we were gone. In-home care was out of the question. I did not want to become an employer having various people in and out of our home or have them cancelling at the last minute when I had an appointment. Coral was showing signs of needing a specialized environment with people trained to care for him.

Our house was sitting vacant, and his car was in the garage as it had not been driven for several months. I knew this would be our home for as long as it took. I had no crystal ball. I just took everything day by day. My comfort level increased, and I felt more secure knowing that, when his condition advanced and his safety became an issue, he would be relocated to memory care and I would be near to him.

Shortly after moving there, I recall our spirits being uplifted when we took the elevator down to the first-floor dining room from our third-floor apartment. The elevator made a stop on the second floor. The door of the elevator opened, and there were about four of the sweetest looking little ladies all chatting while leaning on their walkers ready to descend upon the elevator, laughing and having a good time. Their hair done, make-up applied, it was a picture perfect moment. They looked as if they might be stepping out for an evening at the theatre. It was something you have to see for yourself, as it was such a delightful revelation for us seeing this. I should have snapped a photo to put the image into our memory bank.

Outside the dining room in the corridor were a gathering of walkers like kid's bikes at a school. But here, there were a variation of walkers, scooters, and other assistive walking devices outside in the corridor. All were different colors and sizes, some with little mementos hanging from the handle bars. Actually, it was kind of cute!

Being in senior housing did remove much stress as our three meals were prepared daily, maid service was weekly and some facilities will also include laundry service. There were many activities to participate in, including lectures, entertainment, fun outings to art events and live theatre, etc. There was a van to take us to our various appointments. All exterior doors were locked at night and the security at senior housing was excellent. This feature made a difference for Coral, and he expressed that he felt safe having the doors locked at night. The seniors in the independent part were a very sweet bunch of happy folks.

Being able to walk places was fun for us. Actually, the convenience of living in Ventura was nice, walking to various nearby places as nothing was more than a few minutes away. After all, our lifestyle in Cambria, whenever we went any place required a 45 minute drive to San Luis Obispo or Paso Robles each way.

I recall one morning waking with a very heavy heart when Coral and I first moved into our little apartment in the senior community. We received a phone call from our sweet goddaughter, Taylor. She was in town and wanted to meet up. So, we decided to meet at the Thousand Oaks Mall. Coral dressed in his shirt and tie and off we went to visit with her. We had a great time walking the mall taking photos and chatting. We had lunch at The Lazy Dog and dessert at the frozen yogurt stand. That little gal saved a sad day by lifting my spirits. Just that little break in our routine was so up-lifting. I am so grateful for her being in our lives. She is a blessing in my life and she gives me the feeling I am not alone. Although I do not see her as often as I would like, I know she is there for us. I know from life experience that nothing lasts forever and life is always and forever changing. We live in the midst of evolution, until we become the past and the history others read about.

Since moving to a senior community I felt it was time to stop coloring my hair. I had been debating this option for several months and, at some time in your life, going naturally gray is another liberating blessing.

It was fairly oblivious we both took to the community like fish to water. Although we were much younger, or at least appeared to be much younger, than the other residents, we adjusted well and found everyone to be warm and friendly.

Most people there used their walkers or canes to get around, and a couple of the ladies had little dogs and would walk their pets outside leashed to their walker. Doing our best to be helpful and considerate, often times Coral and I would take their dog for a walk to help them out so they didn't need to walk the dog that day. We were living what appeared to be somewhat of a normal life there. This, of course, was new to us and, I must say, we made the very best of our new environment. I made a couple of really great friends who were both in their nineties. We stay in touch even to this day, though Coral and I since left the senior independent lifestyle. They always ask about Coral when I visit them.

Coral and I have always both enjoyed movies. There are many movie theatres in the Ventura area, so we went often. We even found a Regency Movie Theatre, which showed movies all day on Tuesday for a grand total of $1.00 per person. We decided to definitely make Tuesday our movie day for sure.

The community offered happy hour on Fridays from 4:00 to 5:00 pm. They would bring in different entertainers who would sing and play music. Their music was very entertaining, and it was great to hear tunes you knew the words to. We enjoyed that tremendously. In fact, one evening during one of the happy hour events, we asked if it was okay for us to dance. The music was pretty darn good. They said, of course, and that it would be awesome to see a body or two on the dance floor. Coral and I have always loved to dance and have received our share of compliments after leaving the dance floor, especially when we were on our cruises. We even had won prizes from different dance contests in the past.

We did a mean cha cha for the group and some swing and a waltz or two with our usual flair in the lobby where the entertainment was always held. When we finished our little routine, there was a loud show of applause, which, of course, made us feel really good. Not only did we enjoy the dancing, but felt the residents were touched, and perhaps our dancing brought back memories of their time on the dance floor. I do not know who enjoyed it more, the other residents or us.

Coral would bring up returning home, but never pressed the issue. However, in the same breath, he would mention life was nice here and like being on a cruise ship. Most important to him then were those meals that were always ready for him three times per day, and he truly enjoyed engaging with the other residents in the public area.

Actually, life there was a somewhat refreshing norm. I felt the space of the small apartment was better for Coral, as it seemed he was more comfortable and did not think there was a phantom intruder. Happily, he had no more delusions or hallucinations.

We were close to doctors, which was why we were there in the first place. I knew we would not be returning to Cambria together, although he was unaware of this. When he would ask, "When are we going home?" my answer remained the same: "We are here until your doctors say it is okay to leave." And that is the same answer I would continue to give him in the future, even after he entered memory care.

His confusion still continued when he attempted returning back to the apartment. Coral had plenty of good days, which only served to feed my partial denial about his true condition, but confusion was a part of each day. I was always waiting and watching for any hint or reassurance that what was happening to him may not be happening with his behavior. Yet I was still asking myself whether I had done the right thing.

Since I had more than enough tasks waiting for me at our home in Cambria, I devised a plan that just might work to allow me a few hours of uninterrupted time to start that process. After all, since relocating to Ventura, our home sat vacant and unoccupied.

Over the past several years, I had been involved with the California missions. One Sunday morning, I told Coral I would be going to a meeting at Mission Santa Barbara most of the day. What he did not know was I would be driving to Cambria. I could not return with Coral, as I was advised not to since it might only lead to more confusion for him. I had heard stories about people with dementia returning back home temporarily and refusing to leave the house. I left Ventura at 7:00 am and drove straight through to Cambria, arriving around 10:00 am, knowing I needed to depart Cambria around 1:00 pm to return back to Ventura and Coral.

My life was becoming a race with the clock. While at the house, I filled the SUV with items that we needed and packed boxes that the movers would bring down at a later time. I worked like a Trojan in order to leave by the early afternoon. I would phone him off and on during the day to check that he was doing okay. He had his lunch and was back in the apartment watching TV. He was alone and fine. I returned from Cambria and arrived back at the parking lot of the apartment complex around 4:00 pm. I honked the horn. Coral came out on the little deck of the apartment. I was relieved to see him and felt strongly he would be in our unit after my calling him on and off during the day.

I was delighted with myself for being able to accomplish so much in a day—a six-hour drive to Cambria there and back and three hours working in the house. I was beginning to feel like Wonder Woman. That was just a chance I took in order to start clearing out our home and getting some additional items we needed. We greeted each other, and I explained to him the meeting ended early so at the last minute I drove to the house to pick up some things we needed, since I was so close, and he never questioned that explanation.

One day after Coral and I had lunch together in the senior community, I had an errand to run. Coral walked me out of the building to the car; however, he could not understand I was leaving, but he was staying. Nothing I could say made him understand I was going alone. Ultimately, I needed to walk him back upstairs to our unit. I showed him the chalkboard, letting him know the time I would return, and I told him to wait for me as I would be back shortly.

When I returned to the unit, he was nowhere to be found. This was another moment of panic, and there were several more. Thank heaven for the phone watch I mentioned earlier. I called him and located him. To make a long story short, he was outside by the life-sized chess board in the garden of our complex sitting there alone waiting for me. I was so glad to see him. I never reprimanded him for not staying put. I would just find him and say hello or something like, "I thought you were going to wait for me in the unit."

As I said, I called this new life style "on the job training," as you just have to rise to the occasion as events take place. Every day is different from the day before. There is not a bible or encyclopedia, no classes at the community college, or anything else that is a guideline to this illness or how to deal with all the elements of that individual; each case is uniquely different from each other. Even the doctors cannot give you a timeline or helpline. They dispense drugs, and, as of yet, there are none to stop this illness. They have training in a medical capacity, not an emotional capacity. You are on your own for learning what to do and not to do. This is why the support caregivers meetings are vital.

Unfortunately, when we made the move to Ventura, Coral only had the shoes he was wearing. He never once said anything about an alternative pair of shoes. He just put those same shoes on day after day. This is a man who had multiple pairs of shoes. The trip back up to the house allowed me to bring more shoes for him.

Another issue I needed to resolve was what to do with our large dog. I thought this would be more of an emotional task than it was. The only option I felt was to place him in a kennel. Coral and Sammy, the dog, were inseparable, like two peas in a pod. Sammy adored Coral. If Coral was on the sofa watching TV, Sammy was right by his feet. If Coral got up to go to the kitchen, Sammy was right behind him. If I moved from one place to another, Sammy stayed put.

After placing Sammy in a nearby kennel, it took Coral a full week before he even mentioned missing Sammy finally asking where he was. I thought it might have been devastating for us to put Sammy in a kennel. But after a couple more comments saying he missed him, I never heard anymore mention of Sammy.

Sammy was an older dog when we adopted him from the shelter after losing Madison, our beloved lab, to leukemia. She had been only seven years old. Coral felt he wanted another dog. I was hesitant because we traveled so often and he would have to be boarded regularly. The same was true with his Porsche. Coral loved his Porsche almost as much as his wife, dog, and his mom. He made mentioned to the staff a couple of times he would take them for a ride. After a few weeks, I never heard him mention the car much again.

He soon stopped asking about the house, which gave me peace of mind. What was on my mind was when the time came for him to go into memory care, I would need to dismantle our home alone. I was not sure how this would be done. I had put ideas down on paper but was unsure as to how to put that plan of action into effect, as this was a massive undertaking. Returning to our home, even for a few hours, might be difficult for Coral. I knew we would only be there temporarily, but in his mind it could have led to more confusion. So, once we left, I returned, but Coral never did. Having dementia and going back and forth between two living locations can become more confusing with someone with this illness. There seemed little hope of my returning permanently, as I refused to live there without Coral.

Now that we were settled in senior living, I often found myself thinking of the moment it all changed. The small slice of time when my life went from perfect—or, okay, not perfect, but pretty good, at least—to utterly ruined. I could not allow my mind to linger on these thoughts as it was I who had to direct this band of activities for both our futures.

With time, I was able to attend my first caregivers support group in Ventura, which was weekly at the local hospital. I was on my way to a 3:00 pm meeting when I received a call from the director of the retirement community who informed me Coral was on his way out of the building. The director said staff went after him asking where he was going, and Coral replied he was going to meet me downtown. Coral had no sense of direction and no idea where downtown was or what direction to go in. Downtown was not walkable from where we lived. Perhaps he was going to one of the shopping centers.

Fortunately, he was redirected back into the building to our unit, where he was waiting for me when I returned back to the apartment, as I immediately headed back after receiving the phone call. It was shortly after that incident that the arrangements for him to go into memory care were made. This was the first time he had actually left the property in search of me or wandered away from home.

I was unsure if he would have returned, had he left without being seen by staff, or if he might have wandered around indefinitely.

CHAPTER SEVEN

Memory Care

Relief, Resentment, Confusion, and Guilt

IT IS NOT possible to put into words the tremendous amount of apprehension I had about his entering memory care and going into "lockdown." The term, if nothing else, carries the connotation of something criminal or worse. As much as it seemed like the right decision, I was faced with another hurdle of overcoming the stigma of putting my husband in a facility. There may come a point in all our lives when we cannot provide our loved one with everything they need to be comfortable and safe. What we discover at this stage in our loved one's life is that our best efforts are not as successful as our best efforts combined with those of trained staff.

Here was a person who, for all intents and purposes, looked and talked as he had for years. That is one of the hardest things about this illness: you cannot see into their head. You cannot see dementia. They are not stooped over; they are not hurting; they are not in any visible pain or reflecting their illness in any way, except that they are different now. They have the look of a perfectly rational person. They float in and out of who they are, and in the beginning they are as normal in their behavior as you and I. From that point on, I could not be away from him for a moment for fear he might leave the property and become lost. I even had reservations going to the little gym on the same floor as our apartment for fear he would not remember I was still in the building. I could not take a chance that he would wander for one moment again. Remember what I said earlier? This is on the job training: when it happens, you learn what to do for the future.

Suppose he went missing for more than those short moments we had already experienced in the past? I thought about this, and I could not imagine how or what I would be feeling in the event he would become lost for any extended period of time. We all know what it is like to lose an item, but to lose a person? Not even in my wildest dreams could I even guess the tragedy it would cause.

After that, when I needed to go out without him, I hired a person from one of the local agencies to come in and sit with him and they would watch TV together or walk around the building. Coral said it was like having a babysitter while I was gone.

The arrangements were made for him to enter memory care within the next couple of weeks. My to-do list was revolving in my head. I needed bedding, towels, linens, and photos of past events. I needed to buy a bed and a dresser for him. It was important to decorate his room with his photos and other memorabilia. Everything that needed to be done in making these arrangements for him to be comfortable would have to be done on the sly. I was not accustomed to the little white lies or "fib-lets" that are necessary when dealing with someone with this illness.

I had no idea about the task and necessities to be done nor how on earth I could accomplish any of this. I just knew I had to do it and do it then, without Coral being aware of what I was attempting to accomplish. Once Coral entered memory care, he would have 24-hour supervision, medical management when needed, social and therapeutic activities, and grooming assistance.

One particular morning, we had an appointment to see his doctor. After his doctor visit, we drove over to a pizza place. He always enjoyed lunch when we were out.

At that point, I was acting on instinct alone, as I didn't have a clue how I was going to tackle all of it. I had no time to fret, as I only had time to act. We both went into the pizza place, and I ordered lunch for Coral only. I was not concerned about his leaving while eating his lunch, as I could keep an eye on the entrance of the pizza place while in the mattress store just down the block from where he was to have lunch.

I picked this location for his lunch as there was a Sit 'n Sleep store a few doors down from the pizza place in this shopping strip. I literally ran down to Sit 'n Sleep and told the salesperson I had ten minutes to buy a bed. I bought the bed and arranged for delivery on a certain day. I made certain the bed was good quality, and I am sure the sales person thought I was a real nutcase in my haste to purchase and arrange delivery. I returned to the pizza place and sat with Coral while he finished his lunch. He never ask why he only had lunch and I did not. I suppose it never entered his mind. I was feeling a little like a "thief in the night" running around making these arrangements in secret and behind his back in my efforts to do the right thing for him, for us both. After the bed purchase, I went online to shop for a dresser for him. I selected the kind which is an open nine cube storage unit where you place the canvas boxes into the openings. I thought that would make it easy for him to see what was inside, rather than having traditional dresser drawers.

It was necessary to have his room completely set up on the day he went into memory care so that he would feel at home. This was his space where he would be living, and I wanted him to be as comfortable as possible and surrounded by familiar things.

I ordered the dresser online; however, it came unassembled and there must have been a million parts to that thing. I had to hire a man to put it together. The assembly cost more than I paid for the unit. Okay: fine and dandy; it was done in a timely manner. I had planned to put a big wingback recliner chair in his room with a TV. Of course, I had to move these items into his new location while he was having his first lunch in memory care. I could not relocate them while we both were still living in our little apartment together, as he might question my motives.

Putting the TV in his room required making arrangements with the local TV company to have the cable installed. He had the TV for a couple of weeks until I noticed I had to reset it with each visit, as it was not being turned off properly. After a few days, I realized the remote was much too complicated for him to deal with, so later on the TV was removed. People in facilities really do not spend much time in their room anyway, as they are generally engaged in activities, outings, and dining or visiting other residents in the dining/activity room.

Once Coral entered memory care, I had second thoughts about my residing in a senior community. It was not necessary for me to have the services offered there. I was not interested in having three meals a day, so I started looking around for a place to live. I would not be returning to our home in Cambria permanently. I did not want to live there alone: the house was too big, the memories were too strong, and I needed to be near Coral.

I thought the best thing for me would be to rent a place within walking distance of where he was. I looked around the area and found new apartments within a block, but something told me not to get into any type of long lease as my future was unknown. One rental complex said they could work with me and I could have a three- to six-month lease, in the event that I wanted to buy a place elsewhere later.

When we first relocated to Ventura, I had the opportunity to attend the Buena Ventura Mission for Sunday mass at 7:30 in the morning. After mass, I drove around to become familiar with the different neighborhoods. It was fine in the beginning to leave Coral alone and go to early Sunday morning services and also refreshing for me. He would get dressed and go down for his breakfast on his own and wait for me to return from church in the apartment or public area visiting other residents.

I had covered most of the city in my house hunting and found nothing I felt was acceptable for me. So, I was in a flux. One day, I happened to drive to a new undiscovered neighborhood, not far from where Coral was located and found condos for sale, and I loved the area, which I had not explored before. There was a park across the street and it too was within walking distance to many things that I had already become familiar with. The sales office was closed on that particular day, so I jotted down the phone number. When I called the sales office, the salesperson said they had sold all the units and it was rare to have one come on the market for lease or for sale. I was disappointed that nothing was available as it appeared to be a great location. A few days later, I drove by on a Wednesday afternoon, with the idea of going to the sales office. Something told me to go to the clubhouse, where I saw a group of ladies playing some type of game at several card tables. Low and behold, they were playing one of my favorite games, Mahjong. These ladies all resided in the condo development and invited me to play with them on Wednesday afternoons. I was ecstatic to make this one discovery, as I was on the hunt for a group to play with. As it turned out, I started playing Mahjong with the group every Wednesday afternoon. Shortly after I started playing with them, Kathy, one of the gals, told me a two-bedroom unit came on the market for sale. I immediately called the agent to make arrangements to see the unit the following day. I was so excited, but shortly thereafter disappointed as it turned out the unit sold the evening before I arranged to see it. Wow, what a letdown!

I kept a close watch on that unit. I drove by looking up from my car at the unit which now had a sold sign on the balcony. It was in escrow. I had seen the floor plan via the web, so I had a good idea it was a good fit for me.

Every day, I looked at the unit on the web. I studied the unit and arranged my furniture in my mind. I knew I could make it a home. To say the least, I became obsessed with making the place mine. Yes, I was breaking the law as I was stalking this property. The size, the price, being on the top floor with a lovely view of the park and city was just perfect for a *widow of a living husband*—me. I kept calling weekly to check on how solid the escrow was, and at that point it was due to close within a week or so. I made my final call on a Wednesday and was told everything looked good and escrow would be closing in a few days.

With good luck and perseverance, late Sunday evening, I discovered on the web the property was relisted once again. The condo was on the market again and the listing agent was having an open house the following day. I called the listing agent that evening, and he informed me the unit had fallen out of escrow and he had scheduled an early open house from 11:00 to 2:00. As fate would have it, I could not go to the open house as that was the day Coral was scheduled to go into memory care at noon. All arrangements had been made, and I could not change them. I also needed to move furniture and other things into Coral's room while he was in the dining room. I spoke with the agent and he agreed to meet me at 9:30 the following morning. I woke with apprehension as to what to do with Coral for that hour or so while looking at the condo.

Now I had to hustle and bustle to add this little activity into my day. The next morning, Monday, was Memorial Day. Coral and I had breakfast in the dining room. My mind was racing. I had to strategize how to see the condo without Coral, as well as relocate Coral over to memory care near the same time.

So, I recruited one of my sweet little 90-year-old neighbors also in the dining room to be Coral's companion and wait with him for an hour. She promised not to let him out of her sight. She kept him engaged in conversation the entire time.

I zipped over to meet the agent, as the condo was only a few minutes away. When the agent opened the door, I was immediately entranced by the wonderful view overlooking the green park and the hills of Ventura, the city lights and a peek of the Pacific Ocean—more than I expected. The light of the morning sun streaming into the living area was bright and inviting. I walked through the unit and all I could say to the agent was, "It is perfect for me." I informed him he could cancel the open house and go have a holiday with his wife. I was purchasing the unit. He took my deposit check and scheduled a meeting in his office to sign the purchase documents later that same afternoon. That is how I came to buy and rent and have not regretted for one moment having done things as I had. What a super great community I later discovered I had moved into. So many enjoyable people and events galore going on. I hit the mother lode! What a blessing on that day of all days. I was so worried about Coral going into memory care. The purchase of the condo experience temporarily helped divert my thinking away from Coral's going into memory care. Then again, as ironic as it may sound, we both found new homes on the same day.

This was the beginning of something I started realizing was entering my life, and it is called *divine intervention*. I did not fully comprehend this until I reflected back on the events much later. The Lord was with me every step of the way. He just kept opening the doors. I could not ever in my wildest imagination have done any of these things without him.

I rushed back to the apartment, where Winnie was sitting in the lobby with Coral. She said he tried to leave a couple of times, but she engaged him in conversation and he stayed put. What a sweetheart she was for helping me out for an hour in a moment of need. These little miracles that surfaced in my life were the hand of the one above. All I can say is, "Thank you, Lord, you did it again. You opened the door before I ever knocked." This was just one of many blessings I experienced during this journey.

After the exciting events of the morning, I was ready to take Coral over to memory care, where he joined other talkative higher functioning people for lunch. His room was almost fully arranged and in order, except for the TV and a few other furnishings that I needed to move into his room from the apartment. I had to move these heavy items alone without the help of any staff. The director of the facility did not like the staff helping people move from one building to another in any shape, form, or fashion; I never could understand that policy. That was the management there, and it sucked, and the director sucked. That is why we eventually left. Few people cared for the director, but overall the place itself was great. That is another story for later, however. In fact, funny as it is, I later met several people who started out at that location and later they moved or removed their loved one. Hmmm, I wonder why?

While Coral was having lunch and being introduced to his new environment, I managed to get the remainder of the items into his room. I still have the bruises on my legs from that move that I accomplished alone. His bed was already set up as it was delivered a few days before. All the photos with his colleagues from the hospital and canvases of serene seascapes that I had painted were hung on the walls. There were photos of us together in fun times, wall decorations, and a clock of "Rosie the Riveter." His clothes were hanging in the closet, and his linens were folded and placed in the bins. I wanted to capture and recreate the same mood to make his space as home-like as possible.

After I finished decorating and setting up Coral's space, I went to the real estate office to sign the purchase documents. I returned back to the facility and found Coral in the dining room. This was around 4:00 pm. I escorted him to his room. I said, "Coral, this is your space. This is where you will be while we are here seeing your doctors."

He looked around and, with a sweet smile, remarked about how nice it was, and he would be comfortable here. He thanked me for setting up everything so nicely. He actually thanked me. In my anxiety, I was not expecting this reaction from him. I thought perhaps he might question what was happening, but he did not: he just thanked me. Was he oblivious to the situation, or did he have some level of understanding? I will never know that answer. I just know I had such gratitude for his level of understanding and acceptance.

After a while, I left him there alone as he seemed to have accepted his new location as normal and he never questioned anything. He was happy that I was just across the way and near to him. The blessing is that even after he moved from this location, he continued to think I was just across the way from him. That gave a tremendous amount of comfort to both of us.

I thought he might be angry or upset that he was here under these circumstances, but it was like he understood. There was no resistance, just acceptance. He made it easy, and I felt my plan must have been timely after all, and I had done what was right. This was another little miracle: divine intervention.

After an eventful day of purchasing a condo as well as getting Coral in memory care, I fell into bed when I returned to the apartment. I did not realize these past months had been so draining both physically and emotionally beyond anything I had ever dealt with before. I was made aware at that moment my body ached as if I had the flu. I slept for two days straight. I hardly had the energy to leave the bed and certainly had none to go down to the dining room for my meals. I had my dinner sent up to my room. *I was exhausted beyond belief.*

Guilt was flooding in—guilt at being human and having desires and needs of one's own. Health and survival can come to seem like acts of infidelity, to have a space for oneself a betrayal.

I was treading the quicksand of being placed between the abandonment of self in the name of love and duty and the unyielding protection of self in the name of survival. I felt sick and paralyzed with grief. No one told me that grief felt like fear. Fear of the unknown without Coral. There was sort of an invisible blanket between his world and mine. I was now truly alone; the act of living would be different from now on without my partner.

To mourn someone who has not died yet is a kind of death.

After a while, I attended several meetings at the local church offering grief support. My life felt as though I had experienced a death, a divorce, a separation. What is the difference as you are split from that person who you have been attached to for so many years? We can't predict how grief will show itself to us until it strikes. I just knew my heart was ripped apart by grief.

My heart was heavy, but I knew I needed to leap into gear, this had to pass, and I had to use whatever constructive resource I had to move forward with all that needed to be done. This was just the beginning, there would be many more steps to be taken with all the endeavors to be undertaken. I had to rise above grief to be the foot soldier that I needed to be and Coral would want me to be.

I was living with the emotions of *relief* that he was in a safe place, *resentment* that this illness had taken him from me, *confusion* about everything, and *guilt* of what had to be done.

Doing the impossible to keep Coral at my side, whether here or in Cambria, had become just that—*impossible*. Such a drastic change in our circumstance after so many years shared together, resonates throughout a family, creating concern not only about the care their loved one will receive, but also about the many emotionally charged issues that the move does not seem to resolve. I am so grateful that I listened to my head and not my heart, but I knew my heart was in the right place. I am also so grateful I took the advice of those who could offer support in what I should say and do during these trying times. It is not easy to get over the emotional reaction of moving a family member into memory care. I felt alone and vulnerable.

It was up to me to realize it was a blessing to have that peace of mind that no matter what time of day it was, Coral was being checked on and cared for. It was now necessary to look to others for the help I needed for someone I loved and could no longer help by myself.

The facility had asked me not to come around for a few days to enable him to acclimate to his new environment. This is typical. In many ways, it was a relief, but it was also disconcerting. I could call and check on him, of course. This did not feel like something I should be doing. I knew in my heart of hearts it was for the very best and the safest place for him, a protective place.

After the so-called "staying away" period ended, I visited him every single day. I insisted on doing his laundry myself, as it gave me a personal connection to him. I would take his dress shirts to the laundry so they would be pressed as he liked to wear them. I did everything as I had done for years, not realizing at the time none of this was necessary. I thought I was doing this for him, but maybe I was doing this for my own benefit.

I participated in various activities in the beginning, like the art classes, music, singing, and group walks around the building with other residents. I believe I did these things attempting to maintain that connection to him, perhaps offering both of us some degree of nearness and comfort.

I would sit with him most evenings at dinner time. I never ate my meals there, as the usual cafeteria style food appeared blah. However, Coral seemed to enjoy the meals. We would often take walks in the evening after dinner, much like those walks with Sammy down to the beach to watch the sunset.

For special events put on by the facility, fancier meals were prepared which were very enjoyable. In the early stage of this part of his decline, the two of us went out to lunch and continued meeting friends for lunch at our favorite restaurants.

We still attended church every Sunday, as I was continuing to draw on my faith and it was just a short walk from where we were. I am so happy we did those things, since now we cannot do them together. His original location has changed. He has changed and circumstances have changed. I followed good advice early on. His safety was *key* and I now fully understood I could not be with him every moment, 24 hours a day. I would lose myself and my sanity in attempting to do that.

With so very much to be done, I had to take each step in this process one at a time. Now that Coral was secure, I needed to focus on our home. It was time to remove our belongings from the house and say goodbye to our past way of life, to our neighbors, and to all the wonderful, familiar memories. I would keep what I wanted and needed and release the rest to the world. Fortunately, there was no pressure and no hurry. It might have been nice to lease the house rather than selling at that time. After all, I did not want to give up everything at once at that time in my life.

There were a ton of things I needed to do in my effort to completely vacate our home in Cambria. I needed to go through papers and documents and dispose of things no longer needed. Now that his safety and security were addressed, I could start that process.

Having Coral in memory care allowed me to have the freedom I needed to not worry about his leaving the apartment in my absences, which had been extremely stressful for me. The senior community offered monthly meetings for caregivers. I took advantage of these meetings to learn additional information about dementia. The shared stories of how caregivers coped with placing a loved one into memory care were very helpful.

Nothing is foolproof. For example, if you are out with a person with dementia or Alzheimer's disease and you need to go to the ladies' room, what do you do? Will they still be waiting outside for you to come out? Perhaps they have gone into the men's room, but have now forgotten how to unlock the stall door to get out. Perhaps that person can use the bathroom but has forgotten how to pull up their pants. These are real life situations that cause anxiety and concern when you are out with a person with this illness. There are many uncomfortable obstacles one may become engaged in and issues may arise when you are least prepared. It is impossible to know what to do in the moment your loved one does something embarrassing or has an emergency. Most of what I learned or experienced is what I would call, you got it, *on the job training.* You will know what to do when it happens. Remember, there are no instructions for what is going to happen next. It just happens and surprises you and the person you are caring for. Because, in most cases, this disease is so gradual as it is progressing that things occur that have never happened before. Now you are in the middle of a new experience in public view, which can be embarrassing for both you.

A caregiver at an Alzheimer's meeting shared her story about a flight she and her husband, who had dementia, had taken. When they were on the aircraft, he left his seat to use the lavatory located in the rear of the plane. He came out and walked all the way back to his seat in the front of the plane with his pants down around his knees. He mooned a lot of people on that flight. Can you imagine how embarrassing that must have been for both of them, and what the other passengers must have thought? Again, *on the job training*. I know I keep mentioning OJT, but it is important to keep that phrase in mind. The next flight, if there is a next flight, she will wait by the door for him to exit.

Traveling can be an extra source of stress for both caregivers and seniors alike. The idea of handling a loved one's limited mobility, chronic illness, depression, or other health conditions while away from home can lead to anxiety rather than positive anticipation. To ensure everyone feels prepared before booking a trip, discuss the hypothetical itinerary before booking and acknowledge any concerns your loved one may have. You may need to know how much luggage and medical equipment you will be traveling with, and the special needs that must be met throughout the trip. It is inadvisable for seniors who are in poor health or in the end stages of dementia to travel. If the aging or ill person cannot feasibly participate, there are several kinds of respite care that can enable you to get away and feel confident that they are receiving quality care in your absence.

Even with the phone watch, I still lost Coral. Once at his doctor's appointment, he had to use the restroom (always a challenging situation), and I said I would wait by the door we had come in, near where we had parked the car. I waited and waited. No Coral. I had someone check the men's room and Coral was not there, either. Oh, boy. What do I do? Did he head out another exit and was walking along one of the many busy streets looking for me or attempting to return home or wherever? I looked all over the building with the help of staff: upstairs, all bathrooms, and all waiting areas. No Coral. I went into the parking lot to see if he was there by the car. No Coral. Now what should I do? It was another spurt of anxiety. Any mother can relate to what I was feeling, the same as if you have lost your toddler. Where was he? I immediately phoned 911 and reported him missing, almost in tears. I described his condition and what he was wearing and hung up. Within minutes of that 911 call, I noticed him on the other side of the street, waving at me. Oh, my: another 911 call to tell them he had been found. I cannot adequately describe these moments of panic, concern, and fear that run through your body when these events occur.

Another moment of "Where is Coral?" occurred: I guess I do need that toddler leash after all. Once, at the mall, it was I who had to use the ladies' room, and I asked him to wait for me outside, and when I came out he wasn't there. I called 911 again—at this point they must have known who I was. They were patient and recommended I call the mall security phone number as the mall has cameras all over. I called mall security, who said a security guard would meet me and we would proceed on the hunt for the missing husband. I bet this was not the first time they had encountered this situation. We started our "husband hunt," when who did we see coming down the escalator from the upper level? Yes, Coral, in his green shirt and tie looking dapper and innocent. Another moment of panic for me. I was so happy to see him, and of course did not make an issue of his being momentarily lost. We just continued on our mall walk.

These are just a couple of situations that occurred in our outings and, again, they were *on the job training*. You need to see it can happen before you are aware of it happening.

As ridiculous as it sounds, there were times I would run into the ladies' room always in a hurry, and have him wait outside the door and we would engage in conversation to make sure he stayed close by. Do you feel foolish doing this? *Absolutely*, you bet you do. But it works. Other ladies might have wondered, "Who was the crazy lady in the stall engaging in conversation with someone outside?" The bottom line is, "Who cares?"

I wonder how many people are out there on the streets of cities who have wandered away from what was familiar to them. Lost, confused, and homeless, perhaps with families looking for them. I have heard several news stories of missing family members with this illness. I think that could make a very interesting study.

Mother's Day 2016 was a wonderful day. We had walked to church that morning, and, after church, our friend and neighbor, Maryann from Cambria came to visit us. She had been to Laguna Beach, our old haunt, visiting her daughter and was on her way back up to Cambria. So, she stopped by to visit and see where we then lived. We gave her a tour of the place, which she liked and thought as we did: it was like living on a ship that does not leave the port. She felt the neighborhood with all the shops and coffee house, etc., was nice to have nearby.

At that point, I was feeling truly blessed that I had made the right decision to be where we were. The facility put on a tremendous breakfast and we dined with another resident and her daughter, who would soon be going off to Italy on a holiday. It was fun and fulfilling and overall a really pleasurable morning. Coral and I had a bigger than normal breakfast, so we decided to take a little walk. Afterward, however, when we returned about twenty minutes later, Coral did not remember the brunch we just had and wanted to have another meal. I wondered if he remembered our neighbor Maryann visiting us that same morning. I wondered if he remembered Maryann.

I had to be observant when we went out, as he generally dressed for work and would put on a dress shirt and tie. He always looked marvelously handsome; but very inappropriate for a walk or outing to the movies. Later in his illness and after entering memory care, he started putting on four or five under shirts under his dress shirt. He might put on several pairs of underwear as well.

People with dementia may become paranoid, or aggressive and abusive. This puts a unique stress on any family caregiver, who may be the primary "target" of this paranoia or aggression. Thank the Lord, I did not have this happen in my life. He often told me it was nice living near his sister, after all this time of being away from her. Once or twice, he called me by her name, Beverly, and spoke to me as if I were her, which of course I accepted as the norm. His sister had died several years past, which slipped his mind. He had not spent much time with her and had not seen her in many years prior to her death. He once mentioned to me that I spoke too fast and asked if I would speak slower. Unfortunately, I forgot about that one and think I still talk as fast as I have always spoken.

Charismatic Coral has always had a way of relating to people, and he makes acquaintances easily. I have never known anyone with such compassion and the ability to form such fast friendships. He has a charisma about him so that even strangers take to him and feel instantly comfortable. It was not unusual when he continued engaging strangers in conversation on the street or in stores. He loved to tell people his story or mention to them that he was a physician and they could call him anytime there was a need. He would give them his business card, which was out of date as he had retired some years past. If anyone called the hospital, I am sure the person answering the phone would have said they did not have a clue who Dr. Coral Smith was.

In one of my support groups, I mentioned in the meeting his public socializing and how often he would approach strangers in conversations and give them his old business cards. It was recommended by the group to go to the Alzheimer's Association website as they offered business-like cards to be handed out by caregivers when in public which state, *"The person I am with has Alzheimer's. Please be patient. Thank you."*

Having those cards helped people understand what was happening. Some people would give me a gentle nod as they understood. It made being out and about in public much easier.

Coral staying in memory care allowed me to think more clearly and make some important decisions about our home and starting the process of vacating the house.

When people talk about stress, the unseen reality of life, there are few words that can truly describe stress. And, yes, stress can create many physical problems.

I was exhausted. I cannot imagine how my body managed to stay intact. Energy or not, rest cures all and those two days of rest after Coral entered memory care must have been sufficient. It was time for me to kick into gear for the next "one woman show," and that was sorting out, boxing up, and clearing out of our home in Cambria.

During the "stay away period" after Coral entered memory care, I had what I needed in the one-bedroom apartment, but I could not just let our home sit unoccupied while we were away. His car was sitting in the garage, and there were tons of decisions to be made by yours truly. Since this illness is a one-way street, I was fully aware we would not be returning to Cambria, and I did not want to live there without Coral. Since I am a rather organized person and had more or less organized on paper what I needed to accomplish, now came the time to put my plan into action. The task of clearing out the house needed to be done, and it became a sort of therapy for me to forget some of the stuff happening in my life for the moment. Being a task-orientated person, I needed to do physical work to set my mind in the right direction and clear my head.

Another decision and a major leap of faith was our dog Sammy. Of course, this whole adventure was just that, was it not? My concern about Sammy being in a shelter led me to head east before going north, as Sammy was in a shelter east of Ventura, in Santa Paula. After placing Sammy there, I called them weekly to make sure Sammy was okay. I made up my mind I was picking Sammy up and taking him with me hoping to God I would find a home in the area he knew best, Cambria. My friends were looking for a home for him, sending out emails and letting people know there was a dog that needed a home. I drove to Santa Paula and boldly announced—I lied, or was it a fib-let?—I had found a home for Sammy and was taking him there. The staff was so happy but sorry to see him leave, as he had been a good dog while there.

When we originally dropped him off, I had informed the staff he would snap on occasion. Now, the staff informed me he had never snapped at anyone or any other dog. What a happy surprise!

After giving it some thought, I realized that sweet dog who had been living with us during Coral's illness was in a protective mode, as he knew Coral was ill. He would not let anyone come between him and Coral when they were out on their walks, and he did snap on occasion. Now that he was retired, he could rest and did not have to be concerned about keeping Coral safe from others. What amazing animal instinct! When Sammy saw me, we were both so happy to see each other. He jumped into the car and off we went. I told him we had a week to find a home or he would go back to the shelter, so he had to behave himself. He was such good company for me. I packed multiple boxes during the day and into the night. Sammy slept by my side every night, giving me so much comfort in that big lonely house.

Sammy was a little Godsend doggie while I was in Cambria packing. I was anxious to see if a home would become available for him soon. I packed box after box and got stuff to Goodwill and decided what I wanted to keep and what I did not want. Of course, I could not bring anything back to the small apartment, as there was not adequate space in the one-bedroom place in Ventura. I did not have any definite plans for the future, but just knew I had to get stuff out. That week, I packed over 40 boxes and lined them up along the walls in order to keep things neat and in order.

I walked Sammy each morning and afternoon with high hopes someone would surface and Sammy would find a home and a loving family to take him in. His days were becoming numbered as far as finding a home, and I only had the week in Cambria. I did not want to leave Coral for more than that amount of time. If a home for Sammy did not surface while I was there, it was back to the shelter in San Luis Obispo where we had adopted him.

Packing up Home Sweet Home

A Healthy Task to Clear My Mind

EACH DAY WAS filled with packing, cleaning, clearing out, and walks with Sammy. While packing my mind was racing with thoughts of am I doing the right thing, have I made the right choices? Was giving up living in my home, this incredible location and making the move to Ventura the right course of action?

I was processing and evaluating my past decisions and by the end of my stay at the house I knew I had made the right decision. I was saying good bye to my life here, a place I loved, and it was all okay. My choices were good and timely. I found I was finding strength in my own actions and discovered my own resilience. It was exactly what I needed just then, work that would insulate my mind from my emotional wounds. Human adaptation is miraculous.

Sammy was scheduled to be dropped off at the shelter the next Saturday afternoon, the day before I planned to return to Ventura. One afternoon I received a phone call from a couple, Loris and Glenn, who had two large dogs, and wanted to meet Sammy possibly taking him into their lovely dog friendly home. Another one of my neighbors, Beth, had told them about my desperate need to place Sammy in Cambria. They lived a few short blocks from us. Loris and I met that afternoon so the dogs could get acquainted.

Sammy and their dog appeared to be comfortable with each other. Sammy met their second dog later and it was the same outcome. Low and behold Sammy had found his new home and would move in the day I left Cambria. I was so thankful and so very grateful that Sammy could remain in Cambria where he was familiar and at home. Over the years Coral and I both had watched Glen, Loris's husband, ride his motorized scooter with their three dogs walking along side. The three dogs gradually became two, as the oldest lost its life from cancer. Sammy was embraced even though he was just a mixed breed Labrador and the other dogs were purebred

I guess he was listening to me when I told him. "This is your very last chance Sammy so you must behave or else it is the gang plank for you kiddo". There were even two cats in the home, I wasn't sure if Sammy was going to go for that set-up, but with the aid of his new owners, their love and support he was fine not only with the two dogs, but also the two cats. Later I received a photo of both Sammy and one of the cats sleeping in the same bed together.

We were both extremely lucky he found such a perfect place to call home where he could be happy roaming familiar turf. Sammy's new owners kept me in photos of him romping and playing. A new adventure for him was joy riding with his new owner on the electric scooter. Sammy was happy and loved his family as much as they loved him. This was another act of divine intervention.

So many prayers were being answered under these circumstances. Sammy was not the only issue to be dealt with while being in Cambria this week. Another heart-filled task I had to do during my weeks stay in the house was to get Coral's 911 Porsche Targa relocated to the Ventura/Santa Barbara area to be evaluated to go on the market for sale. I had already called a dealership in Santa Barbara and provided them with photos of the car and they expressed interest in acquiring the car. Coral took such pride and care with all his car, I still see his reflection in the hood of the car as he wiped the polish away. He loved that car. He would keep her clean and shiny. He drove her proudly down the street to show her off. She even wore a hood bra which, was purchased by a secret admirer. Me!

The car had not been driven since January or February the tires were going flat and the battery was dead. This car and all the other porches Coral had owned in his lifetime were the love of his life. The car was always known as 'the other woman' and of course very well kept. No pun intended.

The tow truck driver got the car onto the tow truck and took off up the hill from our driveway. I had tears in my eyes as I watched that car being towed away.

The Santa Barbara dealership had arranged a large flatbed tow truck to drive up to Cambria and truck the car down to Santa Barbara. As it turned out that dealership did not want to give me a reasonable price for the car. I figured they would not factor the sentimental value. And, they would not come close to what it was worth on the market.

When I returned back to Venture I went to Rusnak/ Westlake Porsche dealership with photos of the car and it was Rusnak who made my life a lot easier, as they trucked the car from the Santa Barbara dealership to their Thousand Oaks location for evaluation of the vehicle. Rusnak was able to give me a fair price, the price I wanted. I am thankful for that, as they were very easy to deal with under my emotional circumstances.

How often had I looked out the window at Coral driving up the hill? I would often stand in the window and watch him disappear up the hill when he left home. These reflections on those moments were some lovely memories for me to keep in my heart. He loved that car and it hurt me so to see it leave on a tow truck rather than him in the car behind the wheel. This was just another moment of loss I was experiencing.

I started to reflect back at certain things as being the last time:

- The last time he drove the car.

- The last dance we danced at the dance club.
- The last meal at a certain restaurant together.
- The last walk we would take on the beach.
- The last walk with Sammy together.

So many things were fading away in my life and this was just another reflection of the last time. Another turning point in the emotions one deals with in all of this.

On the bright side, the garage was empty, so I could put boxes where the car had been. Not only was Sammy's situation the good news of the day, but I had more room to store boxes if you call that good news. Hmmmmm. At this point, I am looking for anything reflecting good news in my life.

The car issue was just one of the more emotional things I had to deal with while on my weeks packing adventure, or so I thought.

This particular day I received several calls from the facility where Coral was living. Each time they left a message saying some incident had occurred. Rather than leaving a message asking me to call them, their message left me hanging and when I called them back they were not available. Leaving these messages were stressful enough, but not knowing what had taken place for several hours after receiving their calls was more than extremely disturbing.

Another Michele moment of panic. I did not know if something had happened to Coral. Did Coral do something awful? All kinds of scenarios played out in my mind. The reason I could not reach the proper staff people to confirm what had occurred was because on that day they were at an off-site staff meeting and did not return until after 4p.m. Believe me I was stressed to the max between noon and 4p.m. until I finally spoke with someone at the facility.

Now wouldn't you think they could have left a simple message asking me to call after 4p.m. or just have waited until they were back in the office to call me with their information? When finally I spoke with someone to find out what the" horror at large" was I realized my conversation was being broadcasted over a speakerphone to a totally unknown audience. I was filled with embarrassment and total shock.

No, they in their infinite wisdom decided to leave this message hanging for over 4 hours. I had considered dropping everything I was doing and driving back to Ventura. Had I done that I would have been sitting around until they returned from their off-site meeting still not knowing why they called me in the first place.

Their information was nothing more than an incident between Coral and a female resident. This resident attached herself to Coral like a barnacle on a rock. She, in her state of mind, felt Coral was her husband.

To be perfectly honest, it was not so much the actual reason for the call that disturbed me, but how this information was delivered to me, which was very cold and calculating.

They were well aware I was away for this week working like a beaver in our home as I had informed them. Couldn't they have waited until my return? Couldn't they have been more sensitive about delivering this information?

The lack of professionalism was beyond appalling and showed me the character of the poor management skills and lack of empathy of this place.

To me, it was done like school kids saying, "Hip, Hip, hooray! I cannot wait to tell her." Please, give me a break! Certain circumstances and situations can create a very emotionally charged environment. Under these circumstances is where *empathy*, rather than a lack of empathy, plays a major and key role. There was none of this shown to me, and I am sure other residents and their families have found themselves in the same position as well. Listen, you corporate-run facilities, grow up people. *Compassion* is key to good relationships, not just the almighty dollar.

I think facilities need to understand the emotions the family members are already living with when they are being separated from their loved ones. You would think since they are in this business of senior care they would know how to best handle situations and family matters to make all parties more comfortable and create a more sensitive and positive professional atmosphere.

The facility has the burden to offer sufficient staff at all times to be able to have eyes and ears to prevent certain activity. However, in the event of this "out of character behavior," the facility should use (that word again) *empathy*.

I truly wonder at this point and time if any of these facilities have sufficient, rather than minimum staffing.

Perhaps that is why so many families also have outside staff/care people to be with their loved one at an additional expense. I think perhaps that was another reason for my writing about this issue. I am not the enforcer, but facilities need to offer more to the families. *Empathy*, not just general information, as it costs no more.

After the day's drama, I poured myself a glass of white Zin and started once again packing boxes. Packing was good therapy. I enjoyed having the company of Coral's best friend at my side while I continued this task. Sammy reminded me of the purpose of what I was here to do.

You know a glass of vino always brings a smile at the end of the day or puts a kick in your step and maybe even takes the "bitch" right out of me.

After my week's adventure in Cambria, I drove back to Ventura with the Lexus filled with the precious items for the condo when the escrow closed.

More time was still needed to clear out the house and of course more packing had to be done. Selling at this point was not an option as I had already given up so much and could not even think of putting the house on the market now. Just too much going on and too many decisions to make. I wanted to wait for a better time in the future. I was more than positive I had no interest in returning back to my home without Coral.

My thoughts were how I was going to get the balance of my belongings from Cambria to Ventura. I also had the task of getting rid of the things I no longer wanted to keep, which included furniture as well. An estate sale might be the answer to that. Take what you want and leave the rest for sale. Sort of like another one of my mottos. "Do your best and leave the rest." I wrote everything down in a notebook of what I had to do, but had no clue as it was a mystery of how I was going to get the job done.

My brilliant idea was first to call my dear sweet friend Max, who lived in San Francisco and had spent the last two Christmas holidays with us to see if she could meet me in Cambria. I explained I did not want her to work, but I could use her companionship in that big old "mausoleum," and she could help me decide what to keep and what to leave behind.

I was delighted when she said yes, of course she would offer a lending hand to help. Yay! According to my little notebook, my next step was to give my 30-day notice to the senior community. I would then have the same movers who moved us from Cambria move me to the condo when the sale closed in mid-July. I would be able to move the boxes containing my breakable items from the apartment to the condo in my SUV making numerous trips back and forth after escrow closed.

Laura, one of my new neighbors at the condo who lived on my same floor offered to loan me her double tier cart to make bringing items from my car to the condo easier.

When the movers came there were countless boxes to be moved, and it took them all morning before they finished clearing out the tiny one bedroom apartment. I am a master of packing tight. It appeared there was not much to be moved, but as it turned out there was more than the naked eye could see. Over the years of travel, I have learned to pack 30 days of clothes in a carry-on bag, if you can believe that.

After only a couple of days in the condo and checking that Coral was doing fine, I left again for Cambria. I picked Max up at the San Luis Obispo Train Station. We had lunch at the Apple Farm Restaurant in San Luis which was a good preparation for the long days of housework ahead of us. There would be little time for meals, too much to be done. We literally worked like beavers packing more boxes, clearing stuff out, taking stuff to the thrift shop at the church, having Goodwill pick up items and taking documents to be shredded.

I had no idea how I was going to handle all my art and paintings. Framed oil and acrylic paintings would be sold to strangers at the estate sale at rock bottom prices. Perhaps if I had the emotional energy I could get to know their admirers.

Being such avid travelers we had collected a number of items for our home that needed to be disposed of but not in the estate sale. Some of these things were large and needed to find the appropriate venue. We had two 10 foot tall Japanese wedding kimonos, one a brilliant red and the other white with the crane birds. Each of these kimonos had been placed in custom designed heavy Lucite to keep them dust free and in good condition. They were not only large but very heavy. I had done some checking around and thought it best to donate them to a museum allowing the public to appreciate them rather than attempting to find an impossible buyer, especially because of their large size.

There were also the dozen or so antique clocks that Coral had collected over the years, most of them dating back to the 1840s. My research led me to contact a few clock dealers starting on the east coast, who later referred me to someone in the Solvang area.

This kind gentleman did research and concluded the best price for these clocks at this time would be somewhere around $500.00 per clock at best. Coral had paid substantially more than that for many of the clocks. There was no way I was going to sell them at a giveaway price. Donating them to a clock museum was the only option. I felt it better to have the clocks in a place where they could be seen and enjoyed by others. The clocks now reside in the West Coast Clock and Watch Museum in Vista, California in north San Diego County. These were fine handcrafted items dating back almost 200 years.

These antique clocks were in our collection for many years. Coral would oil them and keep them in tip top shape. Some of them were purchased in pieces when Coral found them and the clock maker restored them back to their original condition. A museum representative would eventually come from Vista to arrange transportation from Cambria.

As I packed up the house, I was aware of the passing of time as the clocks ticked on the walls. These old antique timepieces had so much history, if only they could talk. What had happened in our lives was now history that these fine pieces had witnessed. Now they too would move on to another place in time.

From dawn till dusk Max and I went through spools of bubble wrap nestling trinkets and delicate treasures into packing boxes. We literally were the queens of bubble wrap. It seemed every time we turned around we needed to buy more bubble wrap. Max helped me select what clothes in my closet to take and what to leave for the estate sale.

To help make things as easy as possible I arranged to have the estate sale after we finished packing and had moved the boxes and other things I wanted out of the house. The movers were coming the following weekend to cart it all into the U- Haul that I had yet to rent and figure out how to drive to Ventura.

That was my dilemma before I left Ventura. How was I going to drive my car back to Ventura after driving up to Cambria, as well as, drive the U- Haul down to Ventura with my belongings? Loading the truck in Cambria and unloading the truck in Ventura would of course be done by Meathead Moving Company. Everything I was doing now was a real leap of faith, and in my heart of hearts I knew somehow by the grace of God things would work in my favor in the end. And, sure enough, they did. I was quickly becoming an expert at making plans without the slightest idea how to execute those plans.

It truly amazes me as I now reflect back on what was accomplished in such a short time. I could never have done the things I was doing without the help of the Almighty. He just kept putting the right people and the right solutions in my pathway. I just continued starting what I had to do and things just seemed to work out in the end. There was more *divine intervention* going on than I am able to express.

As it turned out, my neighbors across the street, Steve and Jill came over to offer help. He commuted down to Los Angeles once a month. Steve said if I picked a weekend that he is going down he could drive the U-Haul to Ventura. Jill could follow in their car and even take some things, then they could continue on to Los Angeles, another hour from Ventura. Believe it or not, the following weekend was when he was scheduled for his Los Angeles commute the same weekend as we wanted to depart.

I am so sincere in telling you, so many angels magically appeared in my life doing all of this lending a hand and aiding me in my efforts of what I had to do. The doors just opened automatically and I just stumbled through. More divine intervention.

Once again, I had a plan but was unsure as to how I was going to accomplish that plan in the beginning. I just knew I had to do what had to be done and pray hard that plan might fall into place.

Jill offered to drive us over to Morro Bay to pick up the U-Haul truck, and that was another Godsend. Yours truly, I, drove the big monster truck back to Cambria and parked it in front of the house where it would stand empty until the movers came to pack it full of my things. Max and I were beginning to feel like true women warriors. I am sure poor Max had no idea when she said yes to coming down to help me that we would accomplish so much in such a short amount of time. We were on it and wow, we gals were at the top of our game.

We were lucky enough to have been invited to dinners at friends most evenings as we were absolutely exhausted at the end of each of our bubble-wrapping box-packing days.

One evening Dan and Liz Krieger, super great friends of mine whom I met while volunteering at Mission San Luis Obispo (SLO), came up to Cambria to take us out to dinner at Linn's Restaurant, one of my favorite places to dine.

Dan writes weekly articles for The Tribune newspaper in San Luis Obispo and is an associate professor emeritus of history at Cal Poly State University in San Luis Obispo and was past president of California Missions Foundation. They both are involved with promoting reading and books for children and Liz is a retired Librarian after many years for the City of San Luis. Obispo. In fact, their home looks more like a library as there are so many books lining the walls and table tops.

They transported and arranged for several religious art pieces to be housed in the mission museum. My altars, priest vestment, wooden Madonna statues, and religious paintings etc., as I had been collecting religious artifacts from many parts of the globe over the years. As much as I hated parting with these pieces that were so dear to me, it had to be done. These items were donated to the Mission San Luis Obispo de Tolosa Museum for all the world to see, appreciate and learn of their history. I was so grateful to these two wonderful people and words could never express what Dan and Liz did to help me. There was no room in my new place and I would NEVER consider storing them. I only possessed these precious relics for a while; now, they belonged to the world to enjoy as I had for so long.

At the end of the week, faithful Meathead Movers came and filled the U-Haul which was packed to the brim. Hard to believe the following day they packed what we thought would no way fill up the truck, but as it turned out, the truck was packed to the gills with little room for Steve the driver. We were off and running back to Ventura. I felt I had just about everything that I wanted from the house, and the rest whatever was left, would be sold at the estate sale in a few weeks.

My neat and orderly condo would be filled once again with boxes. The movers met us at my condo after Steve drove the U-Haul down to Ventura and we all proceeded to empty the U-Haul along with the movers. Now Max and I would be unwrapping bubble wrapped items for the next several days. We felt like woman's work is never done, and yes, you can say that again'.

God had answered my prayers more than once as I was doing things I never thought I was capable of. I do not know where the strength to keep pushing ahead came from. I believe it toughened me physically and mentally and gave me even more confidence to move forward. I just wanted to see all this behind me rather than on the road in front of me. I had no time to stop and think about what I was doing because I had to keep moving and doing till the end was in sight and the job was done.

As it turned out it was necessary to make one more trip back to the house as I needed to get some papers and also clear out my office files. With so much to do at the house, we just did not have time to get to all the paperwork. We had just run out of both time and energy. Max was scheduled to take the train back to San Francisco from Ventura, but felt she did not want me to stay in the house alone, especially in its disarray. Out of the kindness of her heart Max cancelled her return train back to San Francisco. She helped me settle into the condo, bubble-wrap and all, and then again we headed up the coast a few days later to do the final clearing out without the high intensity of work that had already been accomplished on our prior trip. There were still papers in my office as I had already cleared out Coral's paperwork weeks ago. I believe we made 4 or 5 more trips to the business office in Cambria to have more papers shredded. I could not just toss this stuff into the trash for any pair of eyes to see.

Realizing I would not be living there anymore and knowing I could not just let the property sit vacant for any length of time, I contacted a property manager to come over and view the home and then look for tenants to occupy the house. I had a time frame of a few weeks to get everything out and ready the house for leasing in the hopes of acquiring new tenants in the near future. Luckily there was a storage closet in the garage where I was able to put some last minute things in there such as family photos etc. paperwork and other items to be dealt with at a later time. We finally finished up and left the house in the hands of the estate sales person. It was a real mess as clothes and household goods were everywhere as items were being sorted out for pricing. If anything, my once lovely home looked like a hoarder's house. It was more difficult to be in the house in this messy state as I am a neat, orderly person, but there was not much I could do about the mess. Thankfully, I would be leaving and not returning for a while anyway. The idea of tenants would be good till I could sort out what needed to be done with my life and Coral's wellbeing.

As luck would have it and more divine intervention, the rental agent, Robin, of Quality Management, already had a couple in mind who had recently sold their home in Encino, California and were looking for a place where there was room to move their massive furniture. Another blessing!

Fortunately, I could not have asked for better people than Brenda and Arnie. They were ideal in my home as they really took such good care in my absence. My property manager was also excellent and understood the restraints of what I could do and not do because of time and distance. She and her husband took on a lot of extras on my behalf and for this I am so appreciative. I left knowing I had a team of people working to ready the house to be leased. No, it would not be as I would have done certain things, but I had to move forward, let go and let others, and I did just that and left things in the hands of very capable people. Not easy for a person like me who oversees things herself. Controlling, well maybe just a little, who knows??

As busy as I was settling into my new condo knowing Coral was settling in as much as possible where he was, I missed him so much, and felt so blessed to be able to have him only a 5 minute drive from where I lived. In the earlier stage of his illness people told me to enjoy doing things with him while he is still able. I truly appreciated that advice as now we can no longer do the things we could do a year ago. I would visit him often and, we went to Sunday church services. We went to movies, although I had to escort him to the men's room and wait outside to make sure he did not take a wrong turn when he came out.

Before Coral's illness was this apparent, we were at the movies and he stopped by the men's room and I went into the movie we were to see. He did not show up so eventually I had to go into several other darken movie theaters and literally call out, "Coral are you in here?" There can be a lot of humility in dealing with persons with dementia in public. Somehow or another we did hook up and we both finally saw the movie together.

After Coral went into memory care we still attended the live theatre to enjoy plays and musicals. I would take him to the barber shop to have his hair cut and a nice clean shave where they treated him with so much respect and dignity. Once his young barber, Diego, asked if he could take a photo with Dr. Smith. I thought that so sweet and kind of this young man to ask for a photo. We continued having lunches out and went on drives to nurseries to see the flowers and to the beach to watch the surf. We even went dancing a few times. He was always a great dancer and my favorite dance partner. That is another thing I will truly miss, my dance partner.

CHAPTER NINE

Things Can Go Wrong

Emotional Ups and Downs of Memory Care

MEMORY CARE IS not an easy choice, but it is a practical one. It was always with a great deal of trepidation when I showed up to visit especially at the first memory care facility. To go through a locked door which can only be accessed by a staff person who has the security code to open the door before I could enter.—it seemed kind of like a high school security prison. But the inmates are allowed to wear their own clothes.

Then, after entering, walking down a corridor not knowing what you might see today. Who might be staring into space or who might be crying out or who might be babbling? Will Coral be at that same door waiting with his clothes in the laundry cart, or will he be in the dining room visiting with other residents? And of course my departing the facility only after a staff person puts in the code and that heavy noisy door slams shut separating us. After almost 50 years that door defines our separation from each other as we are no longer a couple. That door defines my space from his space. I still have the freedom to come and go, he does not. It is sad, very sad. Time helps, but it may or may not heal these wounds.

As Nancy Reagan said this is "the long, long good-bye." It is with mixed emotions when Coral tells me he is happy and actually thanks me for taking such good care of him. True, I feel guilty as I do not take care of him in the traditional sense, but take care of him in making sure he is comfortable, safe and NOT at risk. If I only knew what his thoughts were when he makes certain statements. Does he understand more than I give him credit for?

He has never once asked me why he is living here or why I live someplace else. He has never once said most of these people are older and infirmed. This illness seems to allow him to just be in his environment, his world, his reality without question.

When Coral first entered memory care the first couple of months he would pack his clothes and be dressed and be waiting by the door, but he was easily redirected. This is not unusual behavior when a resident first goes into memory care. I or staff would hang his clothes back in his closet. That behavior lasted about 2-3 months.

He had no problem saying goodbye to me when I left him after our outings, he just walked away with a staff person.

Coral has always been very helpful in doing whatever he could for the staff and the residents. Since his profession was in the medical industry and by nature he loves helping and caring for people, this was his passion. He loved what he did so of course that carried over even with this illness as much as possible. He would tell me these were his patients and he was sent here to care for them. His words in telling me this gave me so much comfort as I knew he felt content and comfortable where he was.

The staff has always enjoyed having him around, and the comments from staff would be, "He is a delight and very helpful."

They said he is a mild-mannered, sweet, respectful man, that description has followed him wherever he goes. These same comments from staff followed him when he relocated to his second facility. He was so helpful and brought comfort to the other residents and a sense of calm. He helped the staff as much as he could under his restrictive circumstances. He added another layer of love and security to the other residents.

Coral and other residents enjoyed washing the old 1940s car in the backyard at Aegis Senior Living, his second facility, and they enjoyed taking pretend joy rides. At one time he started sweeping the patio until there was not one single leaf left on the patio. Even when I came by to take him on an outing he would have to sweep the patio first before we left. It was important for him to have a job to do.

I heard about a nurse who came into memory care, who had nothing to do and appeared bored and unhappy. These people are not depressed many of them may just be bored. The facility gave her a task of walking around with a clip board, something she used in her profession as a nurse, and this made her feel as if she was accomplishing something. This made her happy.

Activities make everyone, whether you have dementia or not, feel important and you are worth something. Being task oriented as I have always been, I am able to compartmentalize and create projects for myself which have helped me to survive and avoid potentially negative thoughts. Tasks do not cure the feelings of pain and grief, but, having tasks has helped me to cope and not focus on the sad events happening at the moment.

With every outing and visit, Coral would greet me with "Hi, I was just thinking about you." That was the very same greeting to our friends and visitors when I brought them to see him. When we entered the parking lot he looked at my car and ask if it was a new car. I told him it was the same car we had for years then he would say it is like a new car. This was repeated with almost every outing. Often he might say "let's stop by his mother's house for a visit." His mother had been dead for a number of years. My answer was always the same which was "perhaps next time we could stop by, but not today." I continued to notice his decline, not so much in his physical appearance but because of his delusions and his moving away from reality.

He might tell me about his fellow airmen who had slept there last night and this morning would be off flying F-14 military planes. He maintained and recalled very vivid military memories when he first entered into memory care. His recollection of the past brought back my reflections of that day many years ago when he stood in full dress military uniform. Tall, handsome, and erect with sheer determination as he had the world in his hands. He was then, and still is, my knight in shining armor. But now, he is a much changed man today than he was that day so many years ago. That is the day I choose to remember this incredible human being.

Since I visited him daily after a couple of months I noticed a situation that became disturbing. A new female came into the first memory care facility and for some reason attached herself to Coral. She treated him as if he literally belonged to her and her alone. When I would come in to visit, she would actually glare at me for tearing him away from her. I was becoming the other woman in his life. We were married, but divorced by the walls of the facility. He had become a part of the community, and this woman was adopting my husband as hers. Coral was uncomfortable with this situation. Coral, being more lucid at this stage, commented about her behavior, but, he wasn't in a position to confront the situation diplomatically to put her in her place. Some of the residents, as well as their visiting families, also commented that she constantly placed herself next to Coral and if he moved away she followed.

The situation was becoming volatile because of her behavior. She would even follow behind us when Coral and I were walking around together.

It was weird, eerie, and toxic.

One evening, there was a party in memory care with the music playing, several of us visitors, residents and staff, were dancing and enjoying ourselves. Other residents were observing the activities but she turned her chair to face the wall so that she did not have to see Coral and me dancing together.

I had mentioned her actions to the staff, who were also aware of her possessive behavior toward him. They attempted to do what they could to keep the two apart. Coral in his state of mind was unable to handle this bazaar behavior he wanted her to stay away, but with her aggressive approach the situation was more than he could manage. It became such an issue that I finally had to look into relocating him from this location. Management had informed me there was nothing they could do. These are not the words you want to hear when you place your loved one in memory care? How dismissive and a lack of responsibility to say this to any family member. This was NOT the place for my loved one.

These answers from management are hurtful and these are the kind of answers that create anxiety when you place a person into memory care. It places you in a no win situation. There are so many changes and other obstacles going on in your life. This offered me no peace of mind.

Finding Coral a new home became another project. I spent hours researching facilities online and driving endless circles to look at them. The interview and inspection process was tiresome. I had little time for myself or any activities.

It was draining and I felt like I was the watch dog (at his previous facility?) The facilities appeared to be fairly well staffed Monday – Friday, but the weekends were short staffed. That is when I spent a number of hours babysitting my husband. The positive side was seeing how Coral interacted with the other residents, playing silly fun little games they would make up. He was comfortable there and I could see how the child-like behavior for him was becoming more prevalent. I am so grateful we had about a year, after his going into memory care of having fun together, almost something of a normal life, although we lived separately. Going places, enjoying dining out, movies, events, theatre and meeting friends out and having friends come to visit him. This all changed after just a short time.

I found a suitable location for him, about ten minutes away by car.

The new facility did their assessment by coming to his current location to evaluate him. An assessment is done each time a resident is considering relocating to a new facility. It is necessary to determine if the incoming resident and the new facility are a good fit. While talking to Coral, you got it, this female resident followed them around and they had to ask her to please leave. She became angry at them and they saw instantly what had been taking place as it was a confirmation of what I had told them. When they first interviewed Coral they thought, "Wow" this man can go into assisted living, not memory care as he was so lucid. However with just a little more time, they realized memory care was the only option for him. It is never easy to be stalked by anyone, especially if the person being stalked has a diminished mental state.

Nor is it easy on the individual who has placed their loved one in a facility. Since you are away from your loved one, the only eyes and ears on that person are the staff people and if they cannot oversee the care, then who will? The Aegis Senior Living staff was aware of the situation and the purpose of the move, they were on guard which made me so much more comfortable placing my husband where there was a watchful eye as it should be under the circumstances. This renewed my faith in the type of care Coral would be receiving. I arranged the movers to come to relocate his furniture and clothes to the new location without any help from the current facility. Yes, another move, how many moves in the last several months? *Many moves*, six or seven—I have lost count.

It was a world of difference going into the new facility-Aegis Senior Living and Memory Care. They invited both Coral and me to join an activity while the staff arranged his furniture and hung the pictures on the wall. What a different in attitude and professionalism. What a difference in management between the two places. Aegis was wonderful for Coral. I visited every other day. When they had special social events and entertainment, we could dance a little and sit and enjoy the music. They offered fun activities such as western night, where we both dressed in our western wear. They had a luau event with fire dances and hula dancers which was fun for both the families and the residents. We especially enjoyed the annual antique car show as Coral has always been a car enthusiast. Because Coral was high functioning he was involved in a number of activities with the assisted living residents. The activity director sent a photo of Coral gardening with some of the ladies all wearing their big sun hats. The important thing here is he was active and enjoying the feeling of doing something worthwhile and productive. This was a healthy environment. I was aware that these activities were great, but later as he diminished, I knew that would change and the events possibly might become too much for him.

Since Coral always wore a button-down dress shirt and nice slacks, he appeared to be a visitor more than a memory care resident. Coral waited by the door and greeted every visitor upon their entry and departure. He would make his escape from memory care into the lobby and the assisted living area, and of course staff in the assistant living part of the facility would see him and easily redirect him back into the memory care part of the facility. He did this several times, but they always observed him doing this and he of course never was able to leave the building. At the new facility he was wearing a wrist tracker, so it was impossible for him to exit the building without them being aware.

Finding the right location for Coral was of the utmost concern for me. You might find it may be necessary to find alternative memory care facilities if the first one does not work out for you. You do not have to settle, if you find the facility is not meeting the needs of your loved one. Find another location that you are totally satisfied with.

Coral stayed at Aegis almost two years, and it was not until he caught the pneumonia virus that things changed for him.

CHAPTER TEN

Late Stage

Worst Nightmare a Hospital Stay

IN THE FINAL stage of this disease, individuals lose the ability to respond to their environment, to carry on a conversation and, eventually, to control movement. As memory and cognitive skills continue to worsen, personality changes may take place and individuals need extensive help with daily activities.

- This stage requires around-the-clock-assistance with personal care.

- They may lose awareness of recent experiences and surroundings.

- They might experience changes in physical abilities including the ability to walk.

- They could have increasing difficulty communicating.

- They may become vulnerable to infections, especially pneumonia.

In October of 2017 Coral went into the hospital with pneumonia where he spent eight frightful days, which included two days in ICU. While in ICU it was necessary to give him a great deal of medication to fight the pneumonia virus. This was hard on him emotionally and physically. It was terrifying for me to witness him in ICU, shaking and shivering partially covered by a thin sheet in this meat-locker cold room as the doctors were trying to bring his temperature down to normal. I was frightened I would lose him. Visitors are only allowed in ICU for a maximum of ten minutes per visit so I could not stay to offer any kind of reassurance to him. When he finally became better and was transferred back to his hospital room he had horrific sun downing. The hospital would call me in the middle of the night to let me know they would have to restrain him and give him antipsychotic drugs. The thought of giving him these drugs was more than gruesome.

He was in a strange unfamiliar place with new faces appearing every day. He needed to have a 24-hour nurse sit in the room since he was a dementia patient. He would pull his IV's out which was dangerous. I could see he was fearful being in a strange place. I went to the hospital every day, but my visits did little to help him feel safe and secure. After eight days he pulled through and was discharged and retuned to Aegis a much different man. This was not a surprise to me, because of his cognitive issues, I expected a different person. I just did not know how much that difference would be. Hospital stays have a disastrous effect on a person with dementia. A frail brain at baseline makes it easier for serious illness to harm cognition further.

In many hospitals, and places of healing, there is an inevitable social isolation that is dangerous for a person whose grip upon the world is already fragile. Put someone in the hospital with dementia, wake them at six in the morning with food they don't like, call them by a name they don't recognize ('dear' or 'love' or 'we' or don't speak to them at all), push pills into their mouth, rush them in their wheelchair down an endless windowless corridor, wrap tourniquets round their arms, put needles into their skin, stand at the bottom of their bed with several other strangers in white coats or green scrubs and stare at them while writing things down with a frown, take away everything that is familiar to them, pull the props of routine from under them, put them in a diaper, just in case, deprive them of the people who care for them and understand their needs and speak their language—and they will suffer and deteriorate and fall away from their old self and often never recover. How about the dementia patient who lost seventeen pounds in six weeks while a resident in the hospital?

He remained his sweet self, but he was much more reserved and less talkative. His conversation became more limited, and he could not relate to the subject. His legs and feet were so swollen he could no longer wear his regular shoes. I purchased house slippers one size larger than his normal shoe size for a better fit. He walked with a slow shuffle step. I knew he was grateful to be back at Aegis seeing familiar faces who greeted him at the door when he arrived.

After his hospital stay, I took Coral to his first doctor's appointment. He was totally silent and it was necessary for me to answer all questions regarding his health care and his medications. Several months before, he would have spoken to the doctor like a friendly colleague. He just kind of stared into space while we were there. He became a person in slow motion, less animated, less talkative and less interested in his surroundings than before his hospital stay.

The medications, coupled with the disease, caused him to become incontinent. The incontinent status added another heavy chain to our freedom and our outings came to an end.

This was difficult for him, and he often became agitated when the staff was attempting to change him. I suggested perhaps it is better to have a male help him when he has an accident rather than a female. He was never one to be rushed and if the staff tried to hurry him he became agitated. Upon his returned to Aegis after the hospital stay, there were a few new staff people which concerned me, as Coral had already been exposed to new faces while in the hospital and I wasn't sure if this would add to his confusion.

Staff turnover is very common in facilities. The pay is low and often staff is not motivated to stay. Many of the young people are continuing on to further education for different jobs. Whatever the reason, the faces often are changing. Over all I was pleased with his care here, but started to think under the circumstances given his current state of mind perhaps it may be time for a different type of environment for him.

I felt he did not need all the entertainment provided and the fancy lunches and other special occasion festivities. I had considered a board and care home thinking perhaps he might feel more comfortable in a home environment. I was not sure and Coral could not offer an opinion.

At his current location, we were being nickeled and dimed. We were not only putting out a lot of money for his room and care, but all the supplies required for him now. The pull ups, the gloves, and the wipes along with the distribution of extra medications caused the costs to climb close to several thousand per month. How long could I continue to pay without wiping out the budget completely?

In most facilities, as the medications are dispensed the cost are based on a point system, one to four are a certain cost and anything over that is an added cost. The more medications taken by a resident, the greater the cost. I felt it was too much and more than I wanted to commit to, after all how long would I be in a position to pay these exorbitant amounts in years to come not knowing how long this illness would last.?

In California, the monthly cost of long-term care ranges from $4,000 to $5,000 per month in an assisted living facility, to more than $11,000 per month for nursing home care. Even home health care is expensive, averaging around $30.00 per hour, the more hours the higher the cost. These costs do not include medical care if necessary and there may not be any reimbursement from your long-term care insurance depending on your policy. Costs across the country for long-term care services are rising at the rate of two to four percent per year. The issue I have with home-care is that you are now an employer dealing with added issues. What happens when, for whatever reason, they do not show up that day, now you have missed your appointment? They have limited hours and any middle of the night emergency you are dealing with alone, when you need help the most.

Having experience and knowledge of the long term care facilities in Ventura allowed me to research many places that might be more favorable for Coral as he reached this stage in his illness.

Since I had become a State Certified Ombudsman several weeks after Coral went into Memory Care and had been working as a volunteer for several months my level of knowledge about long-term care locations helped me make a decision. It is also good to know before life's circumstances lead us into the long term care world, where we have no working knowledge of what is ahead.

For anyone needing assistance when looking for long-term housing the staff at the Ombudsman office in Ventura provides people with accurate and unbiased information and guidance. If you go by the Ombudsman office, you will most likely have an opportunity to meet the resident ducks near their pond outside the office greeting visitor's every day.

Finally, I ended up selecting a wonderful location for Coral. It was a little further for me to travel, but it had and still continues to have an excellent reputation for care and attendance and thus far has worked out wonderfully.

There was just a minimum entry fee unlike many places charging thousands of dollars. Everything was inclusive with the new facility: the gloves, the wipes, and the pull ups were all included in the monthly room rate. They also would take him to his doctor's appointment, and I could meet them there. Since our last visit with his doctor it became a major concern as his appointments were becoming a real challenge for me now. With Coral walking so unsteadily, I feared he might fall and had concluded after our last doctor's appointment that I would need help in the future. So, locating this wonderful place for Coral was good timing.

If you find yourself with a loved one entering memory care, do all you can with them *now* because as time passes all of these activities will become fewer and fewer. That advice from others has proven true for me. Our time out together now is either a visit to the doctor's office or sitting with him where he resides. We can no longer have a conversation of any length but earlier on we could still joke and comment about something interesting, or see something funny and laugh about it. Our conversations dwindled down to the mundane the weather, what was for lunch. Nothing much about the past, nothing much about the future. I am losing my husband in increments slowly but surely. He is losing his lucidity as his memory fades. I still felt an element of comfort when I was with him. I wonder if that is what he also felt.

As the months passed, Coral began to lose hold of the world around him. His short term memory was slipping away. He cannot tell you who the president of the United States is. And his long-term memory was small chats about his military days. Any visitor, in the beginning, might think he is the person he always was, as his appearance was peaceful and so normal looking, but not any longer.

CHAPTER ELEVEN

Reflections of Our Past

IT WAS NOT easy to recognize that while your loved one may look the same, they are not who they once were. My husband is a shell of the person he once was.

During one of my visits with him, feeling a sense of urgency, he got up looking for the men's restroom. He ended up outside the cafeteria door attempting to enter the kitchen area looking for the men's room. I alerted staff who assisted him to the restroom just around the corner, where I am sure he has gone many times before. While he was in the restroom I was talking to staff on the other side of the room. When he emerged from the restroom with the aid of the staff person he promptly went over to sit with another resident. In that short amount of time he had forgotten I was there. I asked staff if I should go over to say good bye and was told it did not matter as he had forgotten that I was present. This illness erases the present short term memory, he may be able to speak of events that had occurred in 1960, but cannot tell you what had occurred yesterday or even five minutes ago. My visits are to make sure he is neat and clean and ensure that he is shaved and his nails trimmed. I arranged to have a barber, manicurist, and dental hygienist make routine visits. It is important for me to know he is as comfortable as possible. He sleeps a lot and often while I am there visiting he falls asleep.

I phoned him some months ago, and he only spoke of a military court martial that was taking place that he was required to investigate. When I said I love you, he paused as if this was out of the ordinary, so I proceeded to talk to him about the military investigation. He thought he was conversing with a military person, who had just said something out of character and too personal. He was talking to an investigative officer about procedure but I was talking to my husband. I have asked myself for months, if he knows me as his wife or as just another face in the facility or a familiar face that brings him some degree of comfort perhaps, who knows? These final stages of this illness are most painful to witness. To watch is to see the mind and body shut down.

Visiting is more difficult now our outings together have ended. I do not really know what to say to him anymore, so I had started to bring picture books or photo albums that we are able to look at together. Once I took his college year book and we both enjoyed looking at the photos for over an hour. I bring my IPad to listen to music, or maybe a movie if he wants, but his attention is short lived.

I cannot feel cheated as I have had one incredible life with this wonderful man. He made a better version of me when we were together.

I need to stay strong as I am the only one who is there to make him comfortable and to make sure he is well taken care of, is safe and as content as this illness will allow. Our lives have changed and I cannot hold on to that part of the past. I can remember the precious moments of the past, but to be effective I need to move forward and view each day as the challenge for what it is and make the most and the best for both of us in a healthy way.

Coral is now in the late stages of this disease, he has lost his ability to respond to his environment. He cannot carry on a conversation as he is losing his motor skills. He may still say words or phrases, but even communicating his own discomfort is becoming difficult to express. As his memory and cognitive skills worsen, significant personality changes are occurring and more extensive help with daily activities is required.

He needs around the clock assistance with daily activities and personal care. He needs help dressing as he might put on multiple layers of clothing, putting on his own socks is impossible for him to do. He has lost awareness of recent experiences as well as of his own surroundings. He has and continues to experience changes in physical abilities, including the ability to walk as he did in the past. His steps are more labored and his feet have become heavy. It has become emotionally painful for me to visit him now. I am sure he does not know me, he is not aware I am there anymore than being a staff person offering him a drink. When I ask him something I do not get an answer from him. The staff tells me he is declining, which is painfully obvious. Today he can pick up the fork and feed himself, but now when his meal is placed in front of him he merely stares at it and staff needs to encourage him to eat. Staff needs to assist him to the bathroom as his balance is challenging and difficult for him. Perhaps in the future he may totally lose the ability to walk, sit or perhaps eventually the ability to swallow. Before he could not communicate a sentence completely. Now he cannot communicate much of anything. He may start to say something, but before he finishes he stops as he can no longer comprehend what it was he wanted to say.

When I leave him I am so over-come with emotions I cannot hold back the tears. This is the hard part, this is not easy on him or on me as I can do nothing to help him. There is no medication to aid him either.

However, medications and non-drug treatments may help with both cognitive and behavioral symptoms but NOT the illness itself. There are drugs on the market, but there is NO CURE and no way to STOP the underlying death of brain cells.

As Coral declines I decline as well. His loss of things we enjoyed doing together is my loss too. Our own very special way of relating to each other has faded away. Gone away. It all happened gradually, yet too fast falling into a hidden recess, a black hole deep and dark.

Are we defined by our relationships? Once those are lost who do we become? We have focused on that person to help make them better and comfortable while; our own loss of them in our lives has concealed the fact we are also losing a part of ourselves.

This insidious disease does not care one way or another. It just destroys all that a person is. It is unpredictable, unfair, ugly, and unrelenting. I have finally learned enough about this disease to know Coral will fade away from me completely with time. Most, if not all of what he has known over his life will disappear. He will disappear from himself and become less than either of us would ever wish on our worst enemy.

I now have not only lost my husband bit by bit, day by day, but lost him to alternative housing. These decisions are *not* easy. They are hard and I alone had to make them. We had already lost another family member to mental illness. Life's tragedies one at a time.

I needed to follow a motto that Coral, of all people, taught me: "I may not like the outcome, but at least I have options," or a saying of mine, "God bless this mess."

As I look back on this time in our lives, I feel in my heart of hearts that I made the right choices. I acted within a certain time line and feel we are in the right place for us both at this time.

Mid-May 2016, I made one of the most difficult decisions I have ever made in my life. I think any future decisions I make from now on will be a slam dunk.

Of course, I felt as if I was abandoning a long-term relationship that had substantially changed over recent months due to his impaired memory. This man is the kindest, sweetest, and most honorable person I have ever met. I owe my own life to this wonderful man. Everyone who met him liked him and he never had an unkind word about anyone. He always looked to the good in people, always left people feeling good about who they were. It is not what you say to another person, it is how they feel when you leave that person.

Why an ending like this for him?

We always said as we aged that we would watch each other and look for signs of deterioration, look for what might not be normal. I guess I never thought about anything more than we would just grow old side by side together in our own feeble way. But, when you are young you feel you will always be that way, until something changes.

I love him from the bottom of my heart and miss him so much! I miss the relationship and partnership that was ours alone. I miss the ideas and thoughts that were generated from him. I miss his inquisitive mind. I miss the fact we would not face the future together as a couple. You know what? "I miss my dance partner!"

I will take care of him in my way to keep him from harm and insure his safety and security and allow him to live out his life with as much dignity and respect as humanly possible. As much as this illness will allow.

Loss that falls short of death is complicated. I am a widow of a living husband as I grieve in the shadows with a chronically ill husband. It is the death of a thousand dreams. There are no rituals for that kind of grief, no poems or tributes, no resolutions.

I have friends who have lost spouses and it is over for them. Mine is a sort of purgatory with an undetermined end.

This is terrible to watch.

I do not like this.

It hurts to see my loving husband like this.

I feel Coral is in a good place. I can tell he is content. He was happy in his last memory care facility also. He is a happy and contented person, which is his personality. I am immensely grateful for that much.

I would like to share with you a very special note from Coral's State Certified Ombudsman, Rik Frye, who visits the facility where Coral is on a regular basis. He wrote:

"Dr. Coral Smith is a lovely resident who is *happy* with his care. He is a consummate gentleman, who is dearly loved by other residents and of course by all the staff. He is talkative; he of course struggles with his memory and orientation, but he has taken his situation and turned it—or, better expressed—he has "seized" this opportunity to serve in his own way as sort of Doctor on call to loving others around him. He would be a rare choice for a dementia resident to come share with our Ombudsman. What we could learn from this *sweet* man in his diminished state."

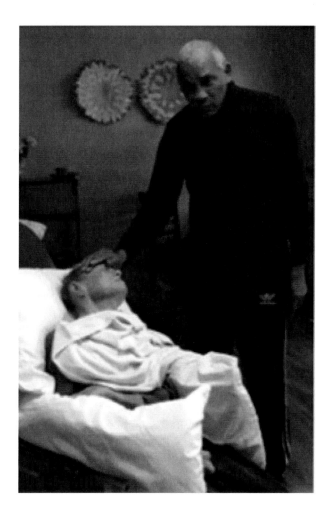

Coral offering comfort by caring & loving those around him

Every time I read this I tear up, but don't get me wrong, they are not the bitter sweet tears but tears of joy, joy for him being him.

Lord, we thank you, even the best goodbyes are oh so difficult. But for those who trust in the Lord, the memory is much more sweet than bitter. How good it is when we can honor those who have served others.

My husband has served so many people in his profession and brought the gift of hope and joy to more people than I could ever imagine. Bless this sweet loving human being for all he has done for others and continues to do today even in his declining state of mind. I know I have seen God at work in everything and everywhere in all of my actions in getting to this point. I look back at the last few years, especially 2016, and I cannot answer how I managed to accomplish what had to be done. But, without *divine intervention* along the way it never could have been possible.

We may not always feel adequate for the task at hand; often we become paralyzed by thinking we do not have the skills, experience, resources, or time to help others. In such instances, we are quick to sideline ourselves, discounting what we do have that might be of assistance to someone else. We use what we have within our own power to move forward.

I encountered angels along this journey. People fell onto the pathways in front of me. They came to my assistance without my even asking. I just stepped out there not knowing what the outcome would be or the answer or the solution. Yet, the goal was completed and everything fell into place as if planned out completely from the beginning.

I always say, "My plan is nothing, but, the plan of the one above is the true plan."

As I read the scriptures each morning, He helps me face a new day, I know he has been with me in every step of this new journey. He has helped me to face challenges while giving me joy, opening doors of opportunity and making new acquaintances and other opportunities.

No matter what, I am eternally grateful for all that I have and all that has been gifted to me by the Lord above. I am not religious, but I feel do unto others as you would have them do unto you. Do the right thing. Follow your heart as it knows the way.

It is difficult for me to comprehend I have thrown open the doors of my private life to share this with strangers. Something in me had to do this not only for myself but for you out there.

Thank you for allowing me to share this journey with you. I am not a commercial writer. I did not know what might emerge when I started writing this story but the words spilled from my heart, to my head and to my fingers onto the key-board. Sometimes I asked why am I writing this, who wants to hear my story? But I wanted to share my experience to show that you can survive after this type of loss. Life goes on and you are still here after all of what has happened.

I worked through feelings, cleared my mind and thoughts, and anchored myself with journal writing. It has given me a way to cope with uncomfortable life events. Writing about the recent events that became a part of my life because of this illness was great therapy for me and not always easy. This diagnosis presented the most intimidating challenge I have ever had to face. I hope I continue to learn from this experience, whether, it is pleasant or challenging.

Becoming a State Certified Ombudsman was important to me after Coral entered memory care. I wanted to grow from this, to learn more and be able to offer help to others in this situation, as well as to honor this important man in my life.

Music is also therapy for the soul and a few lyrics from the song *Yesterday* by the Beatles says it all: Google the words as they are touching. Because of copyright laws, I cannot put the lyrics from the song in this book. This song says it all, so check it out.

CHAPTER TWELVE

Words to the Wise—You

SOMETHING ELSE I found helpful for me to start my day were the many sweet little sayings you find on cups and wall hangings in stores today with thoughts and words such as:

"Follow your heart; it knows the way."

"Today is a GOOD Day."

"Hope."

"Pray More. Worry Less."

"Smile."

"Always Be Kind; Be Good; Stay Humble."

"Life isn't about how to survive the storm, but how to DANCE in the RAIN."

I have these sayings in and around my condo and truly they make me feel good each day to repeat what is written.

I hope you find something in my story that can help you in your journey with this unforgiving illness; if you too are dealing with someone in a similar place.

The Alzheimer's Association is the world's leading voluntary health organization in Alzheimer's care, support and research. Their mission is to eliminate Alzheimer's disease through the advancement of research, to provide and enhance care and support for all affected, and to reduce the risk of dementia through the promotion of brain health. Their vision is a world without Alzheimer's.

Every 65 seconds, someone in the United States develops Alzheimer's/dementia. In Ventura 45 percent of people are living with Alzheimer's disease it is a growing epidemic and the nation's fifth-leading cause of death for those 65 and older. There are almost 200,000 Californians living in Continuing Care Retirement Communities and the need continues to grow. These communities provide residents with the care they need to perform activities of daily living, medication management, social activities, housekeeping, meals and transportation. Some communities also offer dementia care programs and health-related services.

The California Central Coast Chapter is head quartered in Santa Barbara, Ca. with regional offices in Ventura and San Luis Obispo Counties.

If you are considering private pay services through a care agency, here are some questions to ask:

1. What is the hourly fee and minimum amount of hours for hire?

2. Does this fee include taxes, worker's compensation, Social Security?

3. Are your employees bonded? (very important)

4. Are there additional charges for week-ends, holidays or nights?

5. Who pays the employee? Patient or Agency? How often are services billed?

6. What will be the scope of the employee's duties to perform?

CHAPTER THIRTEEN

Recommendations for Caregivers

Take care of your health.

MAKE SURE YOU are eating enough nutritious food and sleeping enough every night. Stress and poor diet will take a toll on your physical and mental health. You play a major role in your own physical health. Accept that responsibility, and take preventive measures.

Get educated.

LEARN EVERYTHING YOU can about this illness and this will provide comfort and reduce stress for all involved.

Ask difficult questions.

CONVERSATIONS ABOUT WILLS, health care directives, and end-of-life care are not fun. It is better to get them out of the way rather than to be left wondering.

Sitting down with your loved one to discuss these things will take the weight off your mind, if you are able to do this.

TALK TO THE doctors so you know what types of medication your loved one is getting and what might be the side effects.

Ask for help if you need to.
BE HONEST ABOUT how you are handling caregiving on top of your daily task. Are you in control or is this situation out of control? Requesting help does not mean admitting defeat. Ask your family for help or perhaps it is time to engage professional help if you feel the need. When possible prioritize what's most important

Plan for "me" time.
CAREGIVERS OFTEN DO not take the time to care for themselves. Maintaining your "me" time will make you more positive and balanced, as well as make you a better caregiver. Perhaps it is reading a book, going to a movie, out for coffee or out with a friend.

Do not forget your spiritual life; this means religion.

For some, it means something else. Follow your faith. It is so important to live in the present, accept the past, and recognize that a healthy present prepares for the future.

CHAPTER FOURTEEN

Resources Available

Resources that may help you in a time of need:

Alz.org/Findus

Alzheimer's Association (Ventura) offers profession-al-level dementia care training for the non-profes-sional caregivers. They are located at 2580 E. Main Street, Ste. 201 Ventura, CA

800-272-3900 (24-hour line).

Coast Caregiver Resource Center: 805-492-0601

Ombudsman Long Term Care (LTC) Services of Ventura County: www.ombudsmanventura.org. 805-656-1986. Authorized under the Older Americans Act, the LTC Ombudsman Program provides advocates for residents of long-term facilities. Receives, investigates and attempts to resolve problems or complaints made by or on behalf of elderly residents of skilled nursing facilities and residential care facilities. The program works to resolve problems of individual residents and bring about changes at a local, state and national level to improve resident care and quality of life.

Ventura County Area Agency on Aging: 646 County Square Drive, Ventura, CA.

(805) 477-7300 or (800) 510-2020 www.vcaaa.org

Assisted Living Connections: Eldercare Advisors, 818-357-1123 or 805-551-1740. When you are looking for transitioning plans for a senior.

Livingston Memorial Visiting Nurse Association: 800-223-4862, www.lmvna.org.

Bureau of Medi-Cal Fraud & Elder Abuse (BMFEA): www.ag.ca.gov/bmfea, 800-722-0432.